# JUSTICE AND GRACE

## BRINGING GOD'S KINGDOM *to* EARTH

# RANDY REYNOLDS

Randy Reynolds is a community developer, counselor, pastor, and writer from West Los Angeles California. He received his undergraduate degree from the University of Arizona on a gymnastics scholarship during the Jesus Movement of the late 60's and co-founded the Vineyard Christian Community in Tucson, AZ. In 1985, Randy started Renewal Counseling and served as its founder and executive director until 2005, during which time he authored and published nine books and workbooks for Serendipity and Zondervan. In 2006, Randy founded Community Renewal, a non-profit Christian community development organization that connects and empowers other local non-profits, for whom he also serves as the executive director. Randy is married to June, and has four children and ten grandchildren.

Published by Randy Reynolds
©2020 by Randy Reynolds
Printed in the United States of America

Cover painting by Patti Triplett
Cover design and typesetting by Cameron Hood
Author photo by Catherine Wills

ISBN: 978-0-578-74260-1

# PRAISE FOR *JUSTICE AND GRACE*

"Randy Reynolds is a *bosbia* to me; he is a hero who has a God-sized vision of rightly-ordered relationships in society in which all get to share in God's peace and goodness. Having adventured with Randy on various projects here in Tucson, I've seen first-hand how his passion and stories, well portrayed here, emanate from the heart of a city pastor who has a longing for God's healing and just community. In this thoughtful overview on justice you will do more than learn. This book will light a flame in you to become a *bosbia*, a godly hero, for those near you that you might not have noticed before. God sees them; God hears the groans of the oppressed, disadvantaged, and lost. And God sees how you can be a hero in His Kingdom call!"

—DR. ANDREW ROSS
Senior Pastor, Northminster Presbyterian Church, Tucson, AZ

"Do we realize the overwhelming number of men and women who are incarcerated in prisons in this country who have a call of God on their lives? We are reminded of those in our communities who are struggling with substance abuse or other addictive behaviors and those who daily walk among us hurt and wounded. In this book, *Justice and Grace: Bringing God's Kingdom to Earth,* Randy Reynolds has presented a powerful and provoking summons to the body of Christ to collaborate in pursuing justice, restoration, and reconciliation on behalf of those individuals who find themselves struggling in life. Randy helps us understand the biblical aspects of justice and how the church can assist in delivering heaven's answer to earth. The Word of God tells us that we are to be transformed by the renewing of our mind. Embracing *Justice and Grace: Bringing God's Kingdom to Earth* will be an exciting transformational journey of putting into practice the principles and life experiences that Randy shares with us—a journey that you will not want to miss. How the faith community responds now will help establish a strong spiritual foundation for future generations. Randy invites us to join him on this journey and has provided us with the spiritual tools that we need to implement justice and grace as they relate to the Kingdom of God."

—Rick Stevenson
Lead Mentor, Community Building Strategies, Greensboro, NC

"Justice and grace form a powerful both/and in the Bible that we mistakenly and frequently treat as an either/or. In this very transparent book, Randy 'Can-I-tell-a-story?' Reynolds illuminates his insights into the issue of justice with story after story of justice being lived out powerfully. Randy's reputation for loving the least, the last, and the lost is well-known throughout our community, and yet even those of us who've walked closely with Randy for years are given new treasures in his latest book. Thank you, Randy, for your faithful proclamation and story-telling!"

—David Drum
J17 Ministries, Tucson, AZ

"Simply put, Mr. Reynolds gets it! This book is a must-read for anyone interested in a biblical approach to addressing the issue of justice. Every believer should read this book and see how it can transform their understanding of justice and grace. For those who think *what's the big deal?* remember that our God is a God of justice and a God of grace. Randy takes the reader from the origins of injustice to solutions that transform. Understanding the perspective of different ethnicities and the impact of American history cannot be overlooked. I served for 25 years as the chairman of the Prison Ministry and Criminal Justice Commission for the National Baptist Convention

USA. In that capacity I observed firsthand the impact of incarceration on our nation's minority communities and on the families of the incarcerated, as well as the decent into poverty of many affected by a criminal justice system that renders unequal justice. This book will help the reader develop sensitivity to people negatively-impacted by injustice in various aspects of life. This book is a challenge to the body of Christ to become change-agents in the pursuit of the principle that 'all men are created equal' as recorded in the US constitution. Read this book and then become a part of the solution."

—D. Grady Scott
Pastor, Grace Temple Baptist Church, Tucson, AZ
Moderator Southern AZ Baptist District Association

"As a single mother raising men—black men—I have experienced injustice: injustice on the part of the criminal justice system, the educational system, and the health care system. I have also experienced God's grace in all those areas as well. In all the cases, it took one person that wanted to see justice and make things right. What Randy does in this book, *Justice and Grace: Bringing God's Kingdom to Earth,* is take a complex topic and simplify it by sharing real life situations and experiences that I can relate to. You take away from it not just a clear understanding of injustice—in all its forms—but justice and grace in the way that Christ provides. *Justice and Grace: Bringing God's Kingdom to Earth* made me take a deeper look at myself and how I look at a situation. Am I looking at the injustice? Am I seeking justice? Or, can I provide grace? Thank you, Randy Reynolds, for you have truly been an eye-opener to me in all your writings, teaching, and life-sharing. I am a better 'me' after reading this book!"

—Traci Hockett
Office Manager, Grace Temple Baptist Church, Tucson, AZ

# DEDICATION

I WOULD LIKE TO DEDICATE this book to my father, Robert R. Reynolds. He was a fighter, a World War II Marine. My dad admired my mother but struggled with the feminine side of her faith which valued love and security over risk, challenge, and courage. He struggled to find his place as a warrior, a hero in the body of Christ. Mom would tell me to "Be careful!" while Dad would yell "Go for it!" He was a very courageous man who I admired and learned a lot from while growing up. One night, a bunch of teenagers were shooting BB's through neighborhood windows. My dad snuck out the back, captured the teenagers, and held them until the police arrived. Dad liked cowboy movies because the good guys always overcame evil and won the fights against the bad guys. Dad was rough—but a good guy—so I dedicate this book to him. This book is about both males and females who are courageous and do not shrink back from evil, but overcome it with a courageous faith.

# CONTENTS

# FOREWORD

T HIS BOOK WAS ORGANIZED around a grant for restorative justice given to Tucson, Arizona by the Department of Labor. The purpose of the grant was for dealing with juveniles who will re-enter the community after incarceration. The tasks were to help these juveniles experience restoration through job readiness, education, and restorative justice. The people involved would design and implement programs in partnership with the three departments of juvenile justice in Arizona. Linda Leatherman was the leader of this project. Rick Stevenson from Living Waters Church recruited over fifty mentors from the faith community. We did eight two-hour Saturday training sessions to prepare the mentors. We also had a curriculum committee who produced two manuals and these were published for DOL. The project had a one-year timetable, and was meant to develop into a non-profit organization to bring restorative processes to the criminal justice system, schools, and the faith community. According to the DOL, of all the cities to receive this type of grant, Tucson was one of the most successful.

The difficulty in this project is that, like so many grant-driven government projects, continued grant money is needed for success. However, our community has taken responsibility for restorative processes with or without the grant money. After all, the goal was to have the faith community own this in collaboration with the rest of the stakeholders in restorative processes. The following book covers many of the biblical aspects of justice which may serve as an overview for the faith community.

# INTRODUCTION

I STARTED IN MISSION AND CALL during the Jesus Movement. I had a lot of friends die during the late sixties and early seventies and felt called by the Caller to serve Him. The hippie movement brought a lot of chaos and brokenness to our country and I was touched and engaged by the hurt and pain of my generation. As each friend died, there was a feeling of finality that left me empty inside and asking, "Could I have done something to make a difference?" They say that justice ministries often start as mercy ministries. I cared about people being hurt and wounded.

There is a story about "mercy people" attending to people being washed up on shore with wounds and those who cared were nursing them back to health. One day a mercy person said, "I am going upstream to see what is hurting all these people we keep finding on our shores." What he found was abuse, injustice, and the need to confront this evil. Community development work has both relief work—bandaging the wounded—but also development work and systemic interventions, in changing evil systems or injustices and calling them to be more just or righteous. In development work, it is not just about feeding the poor, but empowering them to feed themselves and changing the systems that keep them poor. I helped a grandmother the other day who is on social security disability. She can work some but is afraid to work and have her benefits taken away because of her health problems.

Many Christian ethics have been lost in a post-Christian culture where virtue and character are not as important as success, position, power, and significance. Mission was lost in the conservative church with the church split in the early part of the last century. It is now resurging.

There is a research scientist named Robert Woodberry, who through his research has found that much of the positive development in underdeveloped nations, which moved to establish democracy, was heavily influenced through missionaries that were not funded by their nations. Because these missionaries cared about these people and the rights of these people, they were moved to protect their dignity. They saw and experienced the pain and oppression of the people, which filled them with mercy. They were called to be missionaries to these people groups by God and then moved by compassion to fight for the people. For example, when a white 19th century missionary named John Mackenzie saw that settlers were threatening to take the land of the natives in South Africa, he helped them get an audience with Queen Victoria and secured land protection for them. According to *Christianity Today*, without his compassionate work on issues of justice, the nation of Botswana would not exist. With Woodberry's research, it seems that the "single largest factor in ensuring the health of nations,"[1] is the work of 19th century missionaries like Mackenzie and others who were caring people who therefore stood against injustices. This is a different narrative than has been written about missionaries by secular researchers who focused on the cultural insensitivities of missionaries and overlooked their positive contributions. Oh,

---

1    *Christianity Today* January/February 2014.

Lord, help us to see the good in the works of those following Your will and not just their shortcomings.

****

Over the years, both through reading and studying, and personal experience, I have learned a lot about justice; through attending to the wounded as a pastor, counselor, and community development person. Early on, we did halfway houses for new converts. I went back to school to get a graduate degree in counseling to help those addicted to drugs, alcohol, and sex. We did a lot of building community in our new church through small groups. In one group, we had four women who'd had abortions that year, and we saw that there was damage not only to the fetus but to the woman. Injustice is usually about the powerful abusing the powerless, and what is more powerless than a baby in the womb? Abortion was new to me and I was learning about wounded people—how to bind their wounds and fight the systems that created their wounds. We started the first crisis pregnancy center in our city and the third in the United States. Dr. Ralph Rohr, Jerry Peyton, and Lynn Marry Reynolds were the architects of this ministry and Lynn was the first director. As we journeyed in faith, we were learning what injustice looked like and how to navigate the complexities of creating a just and healthy culture.

****

There are little heroes and heroes of great influence in life. There are men and women heroes of the faith throughout history. Most heroes we only know if their heroics have touched our lives. They are often common people doing their jobs like parents, employers or employees, doctors, firefighters, police, and teachers who overcome evil and work for the common good. In the Old Testament, Israel would turn from God, be conquered by outside forces and become oppressed, cry out to God, and He would deliver them from their oppression. The word *bosbia* is the Hebrew word meaning saved, delivered, or rescued. Sometimes it is even used for a hero empowered by God to accomplish His grace. In the book of Judges, these heroes are the hands and feet of a God who cares for the oppressed. The oppressed are not delivered because of any merit on their part, but because of God's grace which liberates them from oppression as they call for help. "But when Israel cried out to the LORD for help, the LORD raised up a man to rescue them" (Judges 3:9). These Judges are called heroes, as Gideon is addressed in his call to rescue Israel from the Midianites. "The angel of the LORD appeared to him and said, 'Mighty hero, the LORD is with you!'" (Judges 6:12). Gideon did not believe he was a great hero but was empowered to deliver his people through faith, according to Judges 6–7.

There are many other heroes of the faith—George Washington Carver, Harriet Tubman, William Wilberforce, Mother Teresa, Cherie Gray, Bob Coate. Both Cherie and Bob died last year and left amazing legacies in our community. Bob was a businessman, coach, elder in his church, and a great family man who did what was right, not for recognition but because it was right. He had over 1,000 people at his memorial to honor a life well lived. You will meet many new heroes in this book who have taken risks, demonstrated courage, fought the good fight, and made personal sacrifices to serve others and their God—to save those who are oppressed, and to work with the oppressed to experience liberation.

Jesus is the ultimate rescuer of the oppressed and He has called all Christians as His followers to be heroes in this life. Have you ever asked yourself, *If Jesus is to be worshipped and the center of our life, why did He leave? If He continued to do miracles, wouldn't He have more of our praise and worship?* Maybe His goal wasn't just to have us worship Him on Sunday mornings, but to live our entire lives to honor and praise Him. It seems He turned the Kingdom of God over to His followers to accomplish His work. "The truth is, anyone who believes in me will do the same works I have done, and even greater works, because I am going to be with the Father" (John 14:12). We are to share in His glory and honor as we walk in faith and are empowered by the Holy Spirit to do the works He has prepared us to walk in. "What is important is faith expressing itself in love" (Galatians 5:6).

There is a timing to this calling, A baby will not make the high school basketball team, but there comes a time when a calling comes. Will they commit, practice, and work hard to make the team? If, like Gideon, the focus is on ourselves rather than our call, we may reject the call based on our abilities or lack thereof, but the call is still there. We have many different roles and calls, but all faith counts in the Kingdom of God. In fact, we are all heroes or "*bosbia* deliverers" because we have the life of Christ in us!

Many of us struggle because we may not look like the present day heroes ("from the movies"). But the truth is, we are heroes empowered by God and rewarded by Him, if we accept our callings. Many of us are heroes—whether male, as the timid little Gideon was, who, though he was filled with insecurities and doubts found great victory as he trusted and obeyed his God—or female, like the Judge and prophetess Deborah, who is portrayed as a courageous woman of faith in the book of Judges. It is not the believer's natural abilities that make them heroic but their trust in and obedience to their God. As they serve God and come to know Him better, their faith will develop.

Praying that this book might encourage you on your journey as a hero in your context of life.

## WHY, WHAT, AND WHERE

I would probably be remiss if I did not acknowledge in the introduction several elements of why these stories came about. As I said on the back of this book, reformation is supposed to follow revival. The Jesus Movement was the last revival in America, but it was a revival without a reformation. I believe, along with others, that it was because of the church split that divided the church between "liberal" and "conservative" agendas. This split came about early last century. The Evangelical arm of the Church came together in a meeting called Lausanne Covenant. This worldwide meeting of evangelical leaders in 1974 decided that they had sinned. They acknowledged that the Church could not divide out "good news" and "good works" and that we were wrong.

> Here too we express penitence both for our neglect and for having sometimes regarded evangelism and social concern as mutually exclusive... nevertheless we affirm that evangelism and social-political involvement are both part of our Christian duty. For both are expressions of God and man, our love for our neighbor and our obedience to Jesus Christ."[2]

So the issues of justice and the social gospel should be included in the Church's divine purposes. Not just Bible study and evangelism.[3]

As this missional movement began, so did a reformation movement. I learned about this through the Christian Community Development organization started by John Perkins. They were in the business of transforming cities and looked at the "City Church" which included all the local churches in each city. This movement went way beyond CCDA and involved many in the Church! Each

---

2    http://www.lausanne.org/ru/lausanne-1974/lausanne-covenant.html

3    For more information go to http://www.community-renewal.com/resources/Articles

city had specific problems to address. Tucson had huge city problems. We were number one in crime, because of crystal meth use and property crime. There were so many areas of hardship that it was difficult to believe we could improve, especially with such low church attendance.

The passage that gave a vision for the city church was Jeremiah 29:4–7, which many city leaders believed called the faith community to work and pray for the *shalom*-welfare of their city. During that time the City of Tucson asked my organization to pray over the city with city officials on the date of its birthday. There is a small mountain in Tucson, called A Mountain, and we would walk that mountain praying for our city. We knew if God did not bless our efforts there would be no city transformation. Prayer is essential in any move of God and we were called to pray. There were many days of prayer, Global Day of Prayer, National Day of Prayer, City Day of Prayer, along with the Pastors' Prayer Summits. So many of the city leaders initiated and facilitated prayer. We had the leaders of homeless ministries like the Giving Tree and the Gospel Rescue Mission with their people at this city prayer walk. We had the S.O.B.E.R. Project, a ministry to help people find Jesus and get sober, as well as our refugee ministry. One morning we had 17 pastors praying over our city. We had city council members, county supervisors, and state senators there. We were working together to see God glorified and our city transformed.

## HALL OF HEROES

Before diving in to Part I, I'd like to put a few faces to the names of some of my own local faith heroes, including some visual examples of what a city prayer walk might look like.

Author's father, Bob Reynolds (TOP LEFT), and Mrs. Lynn Marry Reynolds of Crisis Pregnancy Center (TOP RIGHT), both deceased. Linda Leatherman, who convened the Restorative Justice Meetings as the administrator of the U.S. Department of Labor grant (BOTTOM LEFT). Founder and executive director of Tucson Refugee Ministry, Cherie Gray (BOTTOM RIGHT).

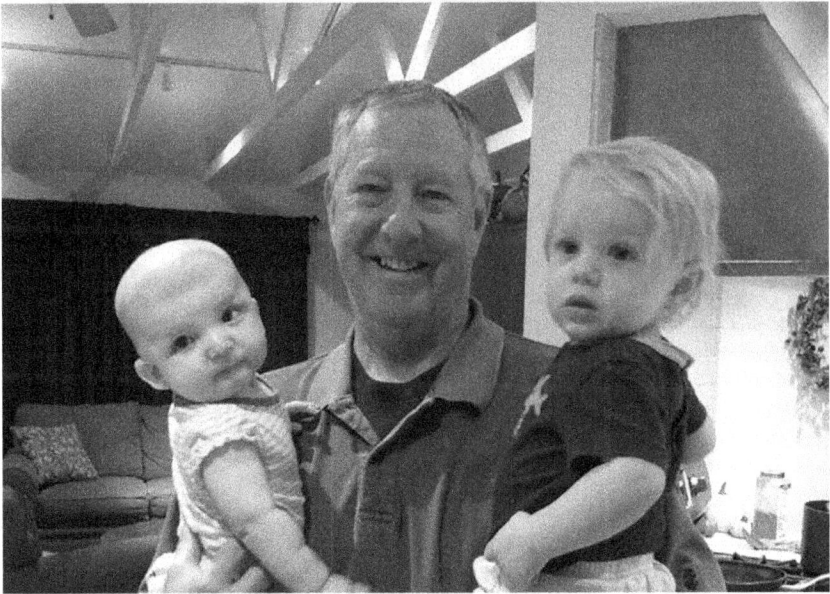

Founder of Sold No More, Jerry Peyton (TOP LEFT). Elder at Living Waters Church, executive director of Oasis Family Center, and mentor-trainer, Rick Stevenson (TOP RIGHT). Local hero of the faith, Bob Coate, pictured with two of his grandchildren (BOTTOM).

The artist whose painting graces this book's cover, Patti Triplett, with her husband Ed (TOP). Founders of Christ Clinic and partners in multiple missions, Jenny and Scott Edminster (BOTTOM).

Members of diverse local ministries come together to pray over the city of Tucson.

# PART I

# JUSTICE AND INJUSTICE

# 1

## FACING OPPRESSION: HISTORICAL INJUSTICE AND THE CALL OF THE KINGDOM

I N MY GENERATION, which was born after World War II, we have all heard about the atrocities of the Germans killing the Jews and the tremendous injustices of the Nazi regime attempting to exterminate the Jewish people. Many of us, however, did not know about the extreme atrocities of the Japanese as they conquered the Chinese and raped their women, tortured their captives, and wrote headlines about who had decapitated the most Chinese in the beginnings of World War II. Injustices of denying human rights and abusing others is a part of human nature, our fallen nature. We are appalled at the 6 million Jews killed by the Nazis, but most do not even know that it is estimated that King Leopold of Belgium enslaved, murdered, and tortured over 11 million people living in the Congo, and then deceptively hid this abuse of slavery, torture, and murder under the guise of philanthropy. In most stories of evil, there are good people fighting injustice. E. D. Morel saw the injustices and deception perpetrated by King Leopold and worked to expose and abolish them for years. Because of his exposure to these atrocities, he took on the burden of fighting for justice. The amount of human cruelty in history does not speak well for the goodness of humanity! Evil flourishes when we are passive and fail to do what is right. To fight the good fight of faith is a call of God.

How many Native Americans were killed as Northern Europeans conquered the tribes of America? An estimated 95% of Native Americans were *eliminated*, and there are horrible stories of false promises, abuse, rape, and the murder of women and children. Historically, there have been so many stories of nations conquering other nations, bringing injustice and abuse, that there is not room enough in this book to cite all of them. The more I came to know about past and present injustices, the more I began to appreciate the call of the King to address injustice. Maybe there is yet something that can be done to help the wounded and stop the deaths.

In the prophetic Scriptures about Christ's coming and His Kingdom, He is bringing justice. It is one of the missions of Christ and His body, the Church. In Isaiah 42:1–4 it says,

> Look at my servant [Jesus], whom I strengthen. He is my chosen one, who pleases me. I have put my Spirit upon him. He will bring justice to the nations. He will not shout or raise his voice in public. He will not crush the weakest reed or put out a flickering candle. He will bring justice to all who have been wronged. He will not falter or lose heart until justice prevails throughout the earth....

There are many stories about people of faith fighting injustice to bring restoration. They often partner with people of goodwill to bring peace and justice to the land. Most of these stories mention people of faith fighting for justice in the context of horrible abuses.

For example, in the book about the Indian wars, *The Earth Is Weeping* a character appears named Brigadier General Oliver Otis Howard. He was labeled odd, but called the "Christian general" and described as a "deeply caring and humane man of genuine faith."[4] Howard, a one-armed general, was given the responsibility to bring reparations and restoration to three million freed slaves after the Civil War. He struggled for years to make progress on this huge task. After that effort, he was assigned to the West where, to the surprise of his peers, he negotiated a treaty with the allusive Cochise of the Apache tribe. Howard had his ups and downs, but he left a great legacy. Howard University is named after him.

There are men and women of faith in most of the historical tragedies of history making a difference and doing good to combat evil. We all know about Abraham Lincoln, a man of faith who was President of the United States, taking a stand against slavery and racial injustices. He believed that the Civil War was a judgment of God for all the years of exploitation of the slaves in America. Many have just learned of William Wilberforce who, with the Clapham group in England, fought and abolished slavery and many other injustices by bringing reformation to England. Wilberforce was a great man of faith and the main leader of the Reformation after the Wesleyan revival. Again, there are too many people of faith to acknowledge in this book—people who have fought the good fight who are an expression of the will of God and the missions of the King to abolish injustice and bring justice to the nations throughout history.

\*\*\*\*

---

4    Peter Cozzens, *The Earth is Weeping: The Epic Story of the Indian Wars for the American West* (Vintage Books, 2016), 181.

I write not just to encourage others but also to help think through my journey. I have always written, read and spoken as a way to seek God and His will in my life. I love stories and one of my nicknames given by a friend is, Randy "Can I tell you a story?" Reynolds. I hope you will enjoy some of my stories in this book.

In the 1980's, I switched from pastoring baby boomers who were broken—because many of the hippies had become yuppies and had grown in most areas of their adult lives—to counseling those who were oppressed by addiction and other family issues. During that time, I met a man who was an alcoholic and had been drinking for 25 years. He was a large man and skilled in his construction trade. Most might even admire his courage and strength in his career. His downfall was women. He was divorced twice and was really afraid of women and especially conflict with his wives. This man would describe himself in the context of conflict with his ex-wife as a man who brought a knife to a gun fight. He, like many of the men I have seen over the years, are avoidant in conflicts with their wives, and his avoidance involved alcohol. He hated feeling bad and wanted to be respected and just feel good. When he would have conflict with his wife, he would leave and head to the bar for a few beers, "looking for love in all the wrong places." What he thought would be an ally became his enemy.

As we began counseling it was obvious that alcohol was what was oppressing him and he needed deliverance and was calling out for help. When he began his journey to sobriety, he would call me up to nine times a day. He started by going to 90 AA meeting in 90 days, but that was not enough. So, he went to two or three meetings a day, if he needed them. Fear and loneliness often overwhelmed him. He was liberated from alcohol's grip on his life as he worked his program, and I had the privilege of going on that rocky road with him. Victory showed up as he received his 30-day chip for sobriety and then his 90-day and one-year chip. He was full of joy as he was free from his oppressor.

## GLOBAL VERSUS LOCAL

In the book of Psalms, there are life tasks given by God. One call is to attend to community issues at the levels of the city, nation, and now the world. Richard Stearns, who was heading up an international Christian ministry attending to the needs and injustices of our world called World Vision, wrote a book titled *The Hole in Our Gospel.* In it he describes how wars and the atrocities of war have torn apart families, communities, and nations. He says since World War ll there have been, "250 major wars fought, killing about 23 million people..."[5] He says three out of four have been women or children.

In our city of Tucson, we see the consequences of these wars. In the past ten years or so we have been receiving about 1,000 refugees a year, washing up on our shores from war-torn countries. Cherie Gray headed up Tucson Refugee Ministry to demonstrate hospitality to the stranger and engage churches in ministries of mercy to refugees. She was an amazing local minister of the gospel, a *bosbia* or hero to many. I did her memorial and saw many Muslims that attended and testified of her love for them. She was the hands and feet of Jesus in our city. As one Muslim leader shared, "Cherie was the first person I saw when I got off the plane welcoming me to this city." I could see how much this meant to him, to be welcomed to our city. Over the years, I've heard many stories where a refugee had their mother and father killed, their home burned, their land taken, their spouse and children murdered. Tremendous injustices by those abusing power. Their stories give us perspective and, for

---

5    Richard Stearns, *The Hole in Our Gospel: What Does God Expect of Us? The Answer That Changed My Life and Might Just Change the World* (Thomas Nelson, 2009) 157.

me, a sense of the goodness of God in the midst of horrible suffering, through people like Cherie who care for the least, last, and lost of our world. Cherie's task was to engage the Church in mission to the world and she engaged many! I believe the Scriptures make it plain that the callings of God are contextual. Richard Stearns was prepared and called to have influence on a global level and Cherie Gray on a local level. What is important is that each person heeds the call of God and serves where they are called to serve, with a heart to please the Caller.

I hope to shed a little light on the call to justice and some of the complexities of this battle. This is a short book that has a particular context of restorative justice but gives a broad overview of justice as a part of God's call.

## SERENITY

Before I start addressing issues of injustice I need to say that they are often upsetting. Life is not the way it should be and accepting or even ignoring the way it is, for many, is difficult. Why address the atrocities of life if they upset you? Why fight for making a difference in a world that seems to be falling apart? For most, hearing of evil or injustice causes an emotional reaction like anger or anxiety which seems to steal their peace. In the Serenity Prayer there is a line that reads, "Accepting this world as Jesus did, not as I would have it." If I get too upset, I become a part of the problem rather than a part of the solution. *Shalom*, working for the welfare of others and the common good of the community, is a difficult task. This book will lay a foundation for why people of faith are called to work towards a more-just life.

On the way to church this morning, a guy in a BMW started riding my back bumper as I was going along in the slow lane. I tapped my brakes to ask him to back off. He swerved around me, jumped out in front, and flipped me off. I was angry at his abuse. The temptation was to act on that anger rather than praying for him. All of us need to be controlled by the Spirit and the Word rather than our emotions, but to have emotion is part of the way we are made. Being angry at injustice or unrighteousness is part of being made in His image, help me Jesus!

Facing injustices and getting involved enough to change things requires trusting God and finding peace with the way things are, even though we are working to right wrongs. Finding rest or peace is difficult because anger is not always sin, but it is disruptive. To be angry and not sin as the Scriptures require (Ephesians 4:26), is difficult, and so many would rather not know about the evils of this world and its abuses. Who wants to feel bad or angry with the injustices in this life? Jesus was amazing in that, instead of acting out His anger, He prayed for those who persecuted Him. He forgave those that sinned against Him. He turned the other cheek rather than mobilizing the armies of heaven to defend Himself. He brought grace rather than judgment. For us to submit to God's will in the face of injustice requires a lot of prayer. We have to work through our emotions so we can represent Christ in facing abuse, sin, and pain. Sins of omission and sins of commission are upsetting, but to do God's will, we have to die to the old self and allow our new identities in Christ to manifest His life in us. Jesus knew that the Father would judge all sin and injustice; therefore, He could surrender, be vulnerable, and do the will of the Father. He found biblical peace and security in the midst of conflict or evil through faith in God the Father. This book is not for the faint of heart, but for those ready to fight the good fight and trust God in the process.

It takes courage and faith to fight this fight. When Branch Rickey, who ran the Brooklyn Dodgers, decided to break the color barrier and invite Jackie Robinson onto the team to fight racism in baseball, he knew he was in for a big fight. He knew Robinson had courage and faith, but he would have to spend 2 years turning the other cheek. Rickey did not want a man who would run from a fight and be a coward, but a man who could stand and fight. He brought out a book called *The Life of Christ*, by Giovanni Papini. In it "Papini" says,

> Every man has an obscure respect for courage in others, especially if it is moral courage, the rarest and most difficult sort of bravery.... It makes the very brute understand that this man is more than a man.... To answer blows with blows, evil deeds with evil deeds, is to meet the attacker on his own ground, to proclaim oneself as low as he.... Only he who has conquered himself can conquer his enemies.[6]

For many years, religion has been more interested in security than in taking risks, with few being willing to fight the good fight of faith, to have the courage to stand in the face of evil and injustice and overcome evil with good.

---

6    Roger Kahn, *Rickey and Robinson: The True, Untold Story of the Integration of Baseball* (Rodale Books, 2014), 16.

# 2

## DEFINITIONS:
## THE DIFFERENT KINDS
## OF JUSTICE

W E WILL LOOK AT the issues of justice and injustice in society, restorative justice, social justice, retributive justice,
and justice that functions within the context of the biblical ideals
of a grace-based community. "Justice and injustice, fairness and
unfairness, reciprocal consideration and exploitation are every-
day concerns of all human beings regarding their relationships,"[7]
says Ivan Boszormenyi-Nagy, a great family-systems therapist
and theorist.

This book progressed from a paper I wrote while studying for
my doctorate. I was originally with a team of people in the area
of restorative justice with juvenile offenders and then became
interested in taking a look at all aspects of justice. As mentioned
earlier this team was really a collaborative effort to help juveniles
with re-entry issues and to help the community with its recidivism

---

7    Ivan Boszormenyi-Nagy and Geraldine M. Sparks, *Invisible Loyalties* (New York: Brunner/Mazel
     Publishers, 1984), xx.

JUSTICE AND GRACE

rates while working towards creating a safer community. It was facilitated through a Department of Labor grant, as I mentioned, because Tucson had the ninth-most juvenile arrests in the country. This book will look at how evil roots itself in individuals, relationships, and social systems and is very difficult to ferret out. I believe that evil exists at intrapersonal as well as interpersonal levels as people interact and create social structures. An understanding of sin or depravity is essential for people's well-being in social settings so they will not be naïve.

## TRADING EVIL FOR EVIL—INJUSTICE

Julie sat in front of me, crying as she told of how her husband had betrayed her by drinking again. He had just finished a treatment program and was sober. They had gone to a party and he said he was drinking non-alcoholic beer, but somehow seemed to become more and more intoxicated. As the evening wore on, he also became more and more arrogant and self-centered, alienating others at the party. Julie confronted Bob the next morning.

"You were drinking last night!"

"No I wasn't."

She knew he was lying to her and she felt crushed by his betrayal and lies!

"Get out! I can't stand to be around you. You lied to me."

"I had to lie. What else could I do?"

With that she left the room, completely disgusted and disillusioned with his lack of honesty and ownership. She then told him to move out. Two hours later he was sitting in front of me.

"I'm done, she is such a bitch! I can't believe she is making such a big deal out of such a small thing. I only get grief and misery from her. I don't think I want to be in this relationship anymore. I've worked so hard to please her. Everything I've done in the last six months has been to please her and this is how she treats me. There is no security or love in this relationship. Why should I even try? One mistake and I'm gone!"

What he didn't know was that she was betraying him sexually. As he had switched his loyalties to alcohol, she was attaching herself to someone else sexually.

Both the husband and wife were justifying their own behaviors by how they were emotionally affected by the other. They were hurt and angry and now didn't care how they affected their spouse. They were trading evil for evil. They did not want to forgive each other because of the hurt and resentment between them. *Hurt people hurt people*, as the saying goes! The relationship was not fair. Evil was taking root in their interactional patterns. Evil was becoming systemic in the relational system. Both of them felt that the relationship had become unjust. They did not want to invest in it anymore because it was not worth it.

All people in social systems create evil—either through sins of commission, omission, or ignorance—and justify themselves if they are not being accountable to God. We all have to have pure hearts and clean consciences or systemic evil will take root. Living in a fallen world means that evil dwells here, and we have to recognize its presence to be able to fight it effectively, even in ourselves. Having a relationship with God through knowing Christ as Savior and Lord is important. Both husband and wife were believers in Christ in this story, but were defeated by the deceitfulness of sin (Hebrews 3:12–14). Emotions such as hurt, anger, bitterness, and fear overcame their faith. This is common in our world!

Today we have factions fighting each other as to who is right and who is wrong. Turn on the TV at night and you will see the unresolved conflicts in social systems—people trading evil for evil. God is not at the center of these conflicts. If each group had humble hearts, being surrendered to Him and His will could help resolve their conflicts. *We can either be right or related,* as the saying goes, and the Kingdom puts the priority on being in relationship. Religion always plays a part in who is right and who is wrong, but religion is not the same thing as faith in Christ and His Kingdom. Religion is pride-based, as is secular atheism. Any time the flesh rules, evil digs even deeper roots into our social systems.

Bob felt he had invested in his marriage by being good, going through treatment to make his wife happy, and there was no reciprocity. Boszormenyi-Nagy describes reciprocity as the basic human exchange that facilitates justice in our lives. "Reciprocity is defined as mutuality of benefits or gratifications, and Gouldner states: 'The norm of reciprocity is a concrete and special mechanism involved in the maintenance of any social system.'"[8] So justice sustains human relationships!

Julie had felt for five years that she had suffered with his alcoholism and was trading good only to receive evil back. She felt this relationship was unjust and lacked a fair exchange or reciprocity as well. It was her time to take care of herself and her needs. Justice or injustice can be found at all levels of human interaction, and without just relationships, we do not have stability. *There is no peace without justice,* as the bumper sticker says, at any level of human relationship. Justice creates safety in relationships, and injustice creates threat, anger, and pain.

A focus on our personal injustices, rather than on God, invites us to be unjust or unrighteous. It robs us of God's grace, which heals torn hearts. It keeps us from forgiving those who sin against us! It keeps us self-centered rather than God-centered, trusting God to bring justice into our lives. It keeps us from suffering well, whether in our families, churches, or communities!

---

8    Ibid., 56.

For our present troubles are quite small and won't last very long. Yet they produce for us an immeasurably great glory that will last forever! So we don't look at the troubles we can see right now; rather, we look forward to what we have not yet seen. For the troubles [injustices] we see soon will be over, but the joys to come will last forever (2 Corinthians 4:17–18).

## INJUSTICE IN ECONOMICS

A few years ago in one of my leadership meetings, a discussion arose about how so many of us had clients that were being victimized by lending institutions. The payday lending stores were giving out micro-loans that were supposed to be of benefit to the poor and were instead victimizing the poor with exploitative interest rates of around 400% annually. The Scriptures tell of how much God hates injustice and exploitation by people who have power and money abusing those without power and money:

> "Suppose he is a merciful creditor, not keeping the items given in pledge by poor debtors, and does not rob the poor but instead gives food to the hungry and provides clothes for people in need. And suppose he grants loans without interest [versus charging 400% in interest] stays away from injustice, is honest and fair when judging others, and faithfully obeys my laws and regulations. Anyone who does these things is just and will surely live," says the Sovereign LORD (Ezekiel 18:7–9).

Payday lenders' intentions were to give short term micro-loans to those who could not get loans because of a lack of collateral, or credit. So, their intentions may have been good. But these unsecured loans also justified exorbitant interest rates because of the high risk associated with the population and type of loan. God sees these predatory loans as immoral.

The problem begins when people focus on their good intentions while denying the evils of their processes. They are still sinning, and they are blind to the harm they cause. Evil thrives when we think we are basically good and miss our sinfulness at work. Depravity is always there. You have heard the saying that *good intentions pave the way to hell.*

All of us at this leadership meeting had stories of people's lives that had been stable and now were undone due to debt. One told of a recovering addict who had been sober for over two years, only to start using again after giving up hope of ever being debt-free. Another parachurch minister told of a man who lost his house and was now homeless because of the debt he owed to the payday lenders. Another told of harassment by the lending institution and how, out of fear, a borrower had stolen from her work to pay the loan back and now was in jail. Most of the borrowers were ignorant of the anti-harassment laws and didn't know, as they were threatened by those doing collection, that they could not go to prison for not paying back these high-interest loans. The borrowers had needs but did not realize the trap they were stepping into in taking out these loans. This was an evil system that led to debt and tremendous exploitation of the poor and would eventually be thrown out by Arizona voters.

It has been said that Christians who have ministries of mercy will almost always have to come to terms with justice and injustice issues in their community. We were being exposed to what was washing the wounded bodies to shore. So many of the wounded have been wounded by injustices, even institutionalized injustice. Those who feel compassion for the wounded now become angry over the oppression and injustices done to the vulnerable. This is true whether you are talking about financial exploitation, sexual exploitation, family power abuse, domestic violence, abuse by business or governments, or any form of abusive power where the strong prey on the weak. So, what is this concept of justice that creates such strong emotional reactions in our lives?

## DEFINITIONS OF JUSTICE AND GRACE

The concept of justice has to do with what is earned or deserved. It also has to do with the rights or dignity of people created in the image of God. The *World English Dictionary*, defines justice as

1. A particular distribution of benefits and burdens fairly in accordance with a particular conception of what are to count as like cases.
2. The exercise of authority in vindication of right by assigning reward or punishment.
3. The quality of being just, impartial, or fair.[9]

Often, when justice is discussed, it is in the context of judgments made for offenses, but it also means so much more. In the legal system, people often want punishment or justice when they have been wronged. The perpetrator owes a debt and needs to pay it back!

I will not spend a lot of time on the issue of human rights as a foundation for justice, but it is a part of the broader concept of justice and injustice. In the legal community, rights are very important and what attorneys often are fighting for. The Scriptures grant rights and are supportive of our rights, but also set limits on them. Galatians 5:1 says, "So Christ has really set us free. Now make sure that you stay free." Freedom comes from the doctrine of creation, the Ten Commandments, and the grace given by

9    http://www.dictionary.com

God, but there are limits on human rights and freedoms in the Kingdom of God. Paul says a little further on in the passage, "For you have been called to live in freedom, not freedom to satisfy your sinful nature, but freedom to serve one another in love" (Galatians 5:13). Rights are connected to responsibilities. With justice, there is always a balance between form and freedom, grace and truth. This balance is found in a relationship with Christ our King. Os Guinness, in his book *A Free People's Suicide*, states that in our republic it is assumed that self-control comes from virtue, which spawns from religion, and is essential for a healthy functioning republic. Freedom can only survive in the context of limits defined by virtue! The assumption of the framers of the Constitution was that freedom could go too far and, as Guinness puts it, kill our form of government. So, justice in support of human rights has limits and also grants rights. There are tensions in our legal system and even in Scripture between freedom and form, rights and accountability.

In 1983, Larry Flynt was sued by Rev. Jerry Falwell. Flynt was the publisher of *Hustler* magazine, a pornographic publication. Falwell led the "moral majority" and had founded Liberty University. Flynt did a parody in his magazine in which he portrayed Falwell as having his first sexual encounter with his mother in an outhouse. He put a disclaimer in his magazine that this was a joke. Falwell sued him for libel, invasion of privacy, and intentional infliction of emotional distress. He won a judgment against *Hustler* magazine. He believed strongly in right and wrong and that moral wrong needed to be opposed and punished. Flynt took the case to the Supreme Court and they ruled that under the 1st amendment Flynt had the right to free speech and, since it was a parody, he could not be held accountable. He believed that freedom was a high value and needed to be fought for! It would seem that Flynt had crossed the line and deserved punishment: he had slandered another person. His right to freedom of speech was upheld and he won the case. I'm sure that God did not approve of his gross portrayal of Falwell's sex life, even if it was a joke. However, a grace was given rather than a retributive justice. Sometimes God grants grace when we are sure that justice should be implemented. "... But where sin increased grace abounded all the more" (Romans 5:20). Paul, who wrote this verse, knew grace. He did not receive what he deserved—justice. Instead, he received grace—that which he did not deserve. He knew the paradox of grace and justice. Faith is complicated because it is more about a relationship with a living God who loves us than it is about values, principles, or even morals.

# 3

## FAIRNESS:
## IMPARTIALITY AND
## BIBLICAL JUSTICE

T HE BIBLICAL WORD FOR justice in the Hebrew is *mishpat*,[10] which has several meanings. It means, "the acquitting or punishing of every person on the merits of the case, regardless of race or social status. Anyone who does the same wrong should be given the same penalty."[11] Retributive justice will be covered later on in this book. However, *mishpat* also means to protect people's rights, to uphold their dignity. There are many biblical imperatives given about ensuring justice especially to people who are powerless.

> Rulers should not crave liquor for if they drink,
> they may forget their duties and be unable to give
> justice to those who are oppressed. . . . Speak up
> for those who cannot speak for themselves; ensure

---

10   Timothy J. Keller, *Generous Justice: How God's Grace Makes Us Just*. 1st ed. (Dutton, Penguin Group USA, 2010), 10.

11   Ibid., 3.

justice for those who are perishing. Yes, speak up for
the poor and helpless, and see that they get justice
(Proverbs 31:4–9).

In the movie *Just Mercy*, a black man is convicted of murder. He is
innocent but sentenced unjustly. Brian Stevenson, a black lawyer
from Harvard Law School, takes on the case to get justice. This
case takes place in Alabama where the rights of blacks were often
minimized because they lacked power and resources. Through
intense effort, personal risk, and sacrifice, Brian tries the man's
case several times. His client has become a scapegoat to eliminate the group's anxiety caused by the murder of a white woman
in this southern community. Anxiety causes people to look for a
scapegoat—the bad person causing a problem—and allows them
to overlook their own contribution to the systemic evil. This sin
of ignorance by the culture was enforced by the police, and it was
empowered by the local white legal system, which was racist. It,
meaning the social system, created an injustice where an innocent
man was forced to go to prison for a murder he did not commit.
In the movie, which is based on a true story, Brian spoke up for
justice and chose to defend the rights of the poor. He won the
case and freed the man.

****

The second Hebrew word that means justice is *tzadeqah*.[12]
It is usually translated as "righteous." It refers to right relationships with God and others and has to do with putting the right
order into our relationships. We will explore these concepts in the
sections of this book referring to social justice and the biblical
ideals of *shalom*. In the Old Testament, *mishpat* and *tzadeqah* are
often "used together" because of how closely justice and righteousness go together in the Kingdom of God. Tim Keller calls *mishpat*

---

12   Ibid., 10.

"rectifying justice" and *tzadeqah* "primary justice."[13] It could be said that primary justice in community development terms is preventative. If all relationships are in the right order, wrong is eliminated, or at least some of it is. When people sin, there has to be correction and restoration in order to rectify a bad situation. In community development work, this is often categorized as either crisis intervention, relief work, or rehabilitation. Corbett, in the book *When Helping Hurts*, says that there is "relief work, rehabilitation, and development."[14] Learning when to do which type of work is essential for health and healing. All of these are important when looking at justice and community development work. We will look at this a little later under restorative justice.

Counseling is about crisis intervention. People come to counseling because they are in pain. Marriage counselors often see couples who have hurt each other and now are organizing their interactions around the pain. They are emotionally reactive because of hurt, resentment, and fear. However, their solutions now perpetuate their problems and they are stuck in a social structure that causes more harm. This is the same dynamic as the payday loans. The solution to the problem now causes a greater problem, a systemic evil of injustice has formed as a bad solution, and has to be corrected or changed or the solution brings more evil and chaos. Justice is to correct injustice, to work on an unhealthy system and bring health to that system. This happens as good is exchanged for evil, righteousness for unrighteousness, justice for injustice, generosity for greed, love for hate, forgiveness for resentment, competence for incompetence, order for chaos, and grace for punitive justice. In this world we are called to work towards these biblical ideals, but know that sin and evil are only completely

---

13   Ibid.

14   Steve Corbett and Brian Fikkert, *When Helping Hurts: How to Alleviate Poverty Without Hurting the Poor—and Yourself.* (Chicago, IL: Moody Publishers, 2009), 104.

eliminated as heaven is ushered in through Christ's reign and the establishment of His Kingdom when He returns.

> Then I saw a new heaven and a new earth, for the old heaven and the old earth had disappeared. And the sea was also gone. And I saw the holy city, the new Jerusalem, coming down from God out of heaven like a beautiful bride prepared for her husband. I heard a loud shout from the throne saying, "Look, the home of God is now among his people! He will live with them, and they will be his people. God himself will be with them. He will remove all of their sorrows, and there will be no more death or sorrow or crying or pain. For the old world and its evil are gone forever" (Revelation 21:1–3).

## EVIL AND INJUSTICE

Most of us have very strong emotional reactions to injustice. When we hear about a wealthy woman who has paid $700 for a pair of shoes living several blocks away from a single mom who keeps having her gas turned off because she can't afford her basic living expenses, even though she works full time, we get upset over inequities. Inequities make us angry. *That is not fair!*

In the story of David and Bathsheba, Nathan the prophet comes to David, who is the King of Israel and responsible for the implementation of justice into his society. David is not only the king, but the judge of the people with the responsibility of establishing the right order of behavior and punishing those who are out of order, so Nathan tells this story to David:

> "There were two men in a certain town. One was rich, and one was poor. The rich man owned many

sheep and cattle. The poor man owned nothing but a little lamb he had worked hard to buy. He raised that little lamb, and it grew up with his children. It ate from the man's own plate and drank from his cup. He cuddled it in his arms like a baby daughter. One day a guest arrived at the home of the rich man. But instead of killing a lamb from his own flocks for food, he took the poor man's lamb and killed it and served it to his guest."

David was furious. "As surely as the LORD lives," he vowed, "any man who would do such a thing deserves to die! He must repay four lambs to the poor man for the one he stole and for having no pity."

Then Nathan said to David, "You are the man!... Why, then, have you despised the word of the LORD and done this horrible deed? For you have murdered Uriah and stolen his wife" (2 Samuel 12:1–9).

Nathan's appeal to David is due to his responsibility to be just as a king. Nathan uses story to drive home his connection with God, Bathsheba, Uriah, and the nation that David was in denial about. He was confronting him on his personal sin. But the appeal to conscience is not about lust or violence, but rather about injustice and inequity. Nathan also confronts him on not obeying God. Kings were not to collect wives, silver and gold for themselves and were to read these requirements daily so they would not become proud and arrogant (Deuteronomy 17:17–20). David's personal sin was pride and a loss of focus on God's will in his life. This led to injustice, lust, adultery, and murder. He also had a lack of compassion or "pity" towards others, especially those with less. Nathan shamed David, and David confessed his sin and got right with God.

David's call as king was to put a "right" order to the social structure of his day. Stephen Mott, in his book *Biblical Ethics and Social Change*, suggests that the social order of the world is fallen and out of sorts with God's order. Satan and his demonic powers play a part in ordering the world and the systems of the world. He quotes C. H. Dodd in talking about the "cosmos" or the social order of the world, then shares his own thoughts: "The cosmos is 'human society in so far as it is organized on wrong principles.' It is characterized by sensuality, superficiality, pretentiousness, materialism, and egoism which are marks of the old order."[15] It is very important that Christians have an understanding of sin and depravity or they will miss or deny evil in their life and the world and not be able to be effective ministers of the gospel. Christians are called to a new order both personally and corporately as they enter the Kingdom (Romans 12:1–2). David was being called to repentance personally and socially by God through Nathan the prophet. He was to face himself and how he had failed to do the will of God, his King. We are called to confront evil and see God's right order become established not only in our own lives, but in the social systems we are involved in (Romans 12:1–2). Every social system has both good and bad in it, but having an understanding of sin and evil helps believers with their callings to do right in their lives.

In the opening story, Bob and Julie's solutions to their problems are sustaining and exacerbating their problems, which is the way cybernetic loops work. They do not know their own sinfulness and they are fixated on the other person's mistakes! Bob wants to feel good, so he drinks, which then invites his wife to be angry, critical, and alienated. She feels victimized by him—not what he really wants in his marriage. She wants Bob to be sober but gets

---

15    Stephen Charles Mott, *Biblical Ethics and Social Change*. (New York, NY: Oxford University Press, 1982), 6.

angry and withholds affection, validation, and sex; which in turn makes him angry and gives him entitlement to drink. He feels victimized also. Both are coming up with solutions that are self-centered and sinful, blaming each other for their marital problems. They do not want to be hurt or feel bad anymore! However, they are now caught in what Mott calls a "vicious cycle, which drives life towards death."[16] That can be a part of many social systems. Marriage and family are the most basic level of social structure in society. Human dynamics are complex and if we oversimplify them morally or ideally, we may just create more problems.

A few years ago, I counseled a single mother who had four children and one on the way. She had begun to get parking tickets and then not pay them. The court system's solution was to increase the fines of these tickets to force her to become responsible. When I got her as a client, she had over $11,000 in tickets and fines. The court was going to put her in jail and take her children away from her. She was driving on a suspended license. Accountability and punishment were the solutions the justice system was providing. She worked as a hairdresser and needed her car to get to work to support her children. Taking the bus would add several hours to her commute and take a lot of time away from her children. She was angry at the court and they were angry at her. They were in a vicious cycle and each side's solution was making the problem worse. She was not an innocent victim of a powerful oppressive bureaucracy but a person who played her part in contributing to the problem.

All of us are sinful, which does not mean that some are not more sinful than others or much more powerful in their abusiveness. However, victims who are validated in their injustices often use those experiences to become unjust themselves. The victims who are hurt and wounded become angry and resentful and use

---

16   Ibid., 13.

their victimization to perpetuate evil on others. They may seek to justify their misbehavior. Volf says, "If victims do not repent today they will become perpetrators tomorrow who, in their self-deceit, will seek to exculpate their misdeeds on account of their own victimization."[17] They had to work together and talk things out, just like Bob and Julie eventually did. The local government is a larger social structure than family, but can have the same dynamics as Bob and Julie in the way that it solves problems, abuses power, and perpetuates evil.

This single mom ended up with her fines dismissed by two different judges. This happened because of a personal advocate, Doris Carlson, who went to court with her and spoke with each judge. Against the protests of the prosecutor, her tickets and fines were forgiven—a grace given. Doris asked me to write a letter to the judges and I spoke of how the legal system was unjust because it ignored context. The judges required she go to counseling and work on taking responsibility for her life and choices. They granted grace/forgiveness and truth/accountability through counseling.

---

17  Miroslav Volf, *Exclusion and Embrace: A Theological Exploration of Identity, Otherness, and Reconciliation* (Nashville: Abingdon Press, 1996), 117.

# 4

## GOOD INTENTIONS
## CAN CREATE BAD RESULTS:
## EVIL CYCLES IN SOCIAL
## SYSTEMS

I N THE LAST ECONOMIC DOWNTURN, the Great Recession, several
systems victimized our culture in the housing bubble. Both
business and government worked together to negatively create a
system that caused the crash. Business lent money for housing
loans to people who could not afford to pay back these loans.
This became apparent when interest rates climbed and so many
defaulted on their loans. Business worked in a very greedy mode
in their lending practices, bundling mortgages and selling them
as bonds. Just like those lending payday loans, they were exploitative, not really caring whether the borrowers could afford the
money they borrowed. Government, as public servants, wanted
more of the poor in their own houses. This policy was called
the Community Reinvestment Act. In their arrogance they overlooked, in attempting to do good through their policies, some very
basic issues like whether the poor could afford the houses they
were buying. There was a concern over justice issues in the area

of redistribution of wealth through property ownership, surely a great mission. They overlooked the buyer's personal competencies and responsibility in the process. Could they really afford these homes they were buying, especially when some lenders were lending up to 120% of the value of the home? Here is what Jim Collins, in a non-religious critique, says of the crash in his book, *How the Mighty Fall*:

> Finally, there's a provocative lesson: beware the hubris that can arise in conjunction with missionary zeal. In the *Built to Last* study, Jerry Porras and I found that enduring great companies passionately adhere to a set of timeless core values and pursue a core purpose beyond just making money. But there is also a risk to manage: having an almost righteous sense of one's values and purpose ("We're the good guys") can perhaps make a company more vulnerable to Stages 1 to 3. Fannie Mae's missionary zeal for expanding the American Dream of home ownership to as many Americans as possible contributed, in part, to its arrogance, its pursuit of growth, and even its increased risk profile. Whenever people begin to confuse the nobility of their cause with the goodness and wisdom of their actions—"We're good people in pursuit of a noble cause, and therefore our decisions are good and wise"—they can perhaps more easily lead themselves astray. Bad decisions made with good intentions are still bad decisions.[18]

This sounds an awful lot like *good intentions pave the way to hell.*

---

18    James C. Collins, *How the Mighty Fall: And Why Some Companies Never Give In* (New York: Jim Collins: Distributed in the U.S. and Canada exclusively by HarperCollins Publishers, 2009), 148.

Many people lost their houses and became very embittered at lenders in our community. Up to 40% of Arizona homeowners lost their homes and many developers went bankrupt. The government bailed out the banks who owned failing mortgages.

Often times, the injustices create hatred because of the victimization. Many become threatened, resentful, and emotionally reactive. When people are violated, they have strong emotional reactions—like Julie and Bob, or King David. However, to fight evil and injustice, we as believers may need to be more objective. We must be able to hate the sin and yet love the sinner.

As believers, we need to know that there are no good guys who are innocent fighting bad guys who are evil. We all sin and fall short of the glory of God. Volf says, "Every person's heart is blemished with sin; every ideal and project is infected with corruption; every ascription of guilt and innocence saddled with non-innocence."[19] That does not mean that there are not people who are weak, powerless, and often somewhat innocent. But if we do not understand depravity, then the religious temptation to self-righteousness, pride, and arrogance can blind us into creating much evil in the name of goodness.

If we understand our own depravity, we will approach others differently. We may be less judgmental and more gracious, but still be passionate about fighting evil and injustice. God created us to get angry over injustice and the evil perpetuated on the weak, but we also will do much better if we can use wisdom, love, and grace—not hatred, judgment, or evil alliances— to fight wrong. Psychologists say we have to externalize a problem rather than internalize a problem in order to deal with it well. Reinhold Niebuhr put it this way:

> One of the most important results of a spiritual discipline against resentment in a social dispute is

---

19   Volf, 84.

that it leads to an effort to discriminate between the evils of a social system and situation and the individuals who are involved in it. Individuals are never as immoral as the social situations in which they are involved and which they symbolize.[20]

When we look at a social system that we all agree is evil, where injustice, oppression, inequity, violence and all sorts of evil exist, it does help to be able to separate out the people who exist in those systems.

Nelson Mandela worked towards ending one of these vicious cycles in South Africa. He was a part of the African National Congress, which fought Apartheid's injustices and oppression with violence. Because of his violence, he went to prison. He was caught up in trading evil for evil. He was oppressed by racism and became very angry and resentful and used evil or violence to fight back at first. In prison he had time to reflect, and that seemed to help him come to terms with his own anger over sin and injustice. He said, "In prison, my anger toward whites decreased, but my hatred for the system grew. I wanted South Africa to see that I loved even my enemies while I hated the system that turned us against one another."[21] Because of his maturity, he was able to help solve systemic evil that had cost many their lives.

In the Christian faith, we have similar reasoning. The Scripture says,

> For we are not fighting against people made of flesh and blood, but against the evil rulers and authorities of the unseen world, against those mighty powers of darkness who rule this world [cosmos] and against wicked spirits in the heavenly realms (Ephesians 6:12).

---

20  Mott, 56.

21  Nelson Mandela, *Long Walk to Freedom* (Boston: Little, Brown & Co., 1994), 568.

In other words, it is not the people who are our enemies but the devils behind the scenes.

## HEROES NEED COURAGE AND GRACE

The call to be a *bosbia*-hero of the faith requires courage. This is something believers are given, but may not naturally have in the flesh. Courage comes through faith in God. The Scripture says, "They [people of faith] are confident and fearless and can face their foes triumphantly" (Psalm 112:8). Why? The verse before this verse says, "...they confidently trust the LORD to care for them" (Psalm 112:7).

The call to stand against evil and be a warrior like King David exposes us to threat by enemies. We are in a battle with unseen enemies who are very committed to winning the fight. So, threat and vulnerability are very real and do provoke anxiety. When David stands before Goliath, he is a boy up against a giant who intimidates his enemies. David's confidence first of all comes from God. David says, "The LORD who saved me from the claws of the lion and the bear will save me from this Philistine" (1 Samuel 17:37). David was equipped, and God similarly prepares us all for works of service so His Kingdom will come to earth through doing His will. Over and over again in the writings of David, God is referenced as the one who helps him to be confident in all his battles with all his enemies.

I have found that most people use themselves as their reference point rather than God. He is our shelter, our safe place even in a battle with evil. His promises and His faithfulness are what grants us faith or confidence when facing our battles.

Jesus has defeated the devil and is our advocate, "So why should I be afraid? So why should I tremble?" (Psalm 27:1–3). Jesus has accomplished so much that empowers us to be overcomers. His life grants us protection and provision that empowers us for the missions He invites us into. What may appear as a threat may only be provoking us to be fearful and anxious, but because of Him we can be confident when facing our enemies. Fear invites us to withdraw, to quit, and the devil is the one behind all fear that confronts and undermines our faith and our calling. But Christ has overcome and will help *us* to overcome and fulfill our missions.

There is a little story of a father and son driving down the road and a bee flies into the car. The boy becomes afraid and starts crying. Dad grabs the bee and holds it in his hand. He then lets it go. The boy screams and the father says, "There is nothing to be afraid of," and opens his hand. The stinger is in dad's hand and the bee is powerless to hurt his son. Christ has taken the sting for us. For all faith heroes, trusting in God grants confidence as they are threatened. He also grants us victory in the midst of the battles of faith.

****

The other emotion that undermines the hero in us is shame. So many of the men I have worked with are still ashamed and guilty and will not step into their callings because of their shame. Our faith is not ultimately about us, but about the object of our faith: Jesus. Our reputation and significance are only secure in Him.

David again is a great example of a "man" who overcomes. He has had an affair with Bathsheba and kills her husband. He abuses his position of power and gets caught while denying his culpability. I have worked with hundreds of men and women who are guilty and ashamed. If they can't find grace and forgiveness in Christ, they will not embrace their new identities in Christ. They will be bound by the devil to an old identity, and a past history that restricts them from their callings. David is called to be King of Israel, but isn't he disqualified because of his sin? He knows that his calling is a divine appointment and not based on the approval of men. David is ashamed of his guilt. He knows that he has sinned against God and it is up to God as to whether he will continue in his calling. Nathan the prophet makes it clear that God will judge sin, but forgives David. There will be difficult consequences for his sinning, but David's confession is what is required to be right with his God.

What amazes me is that David does not quit his calling. He writes two psalms about his sin (Psalm 32 and Psalm 51) and deals with his vulnerability by embracing his shame and guilt in the context of his faith in God's grace. He doesn't quit and continues to walk in faith in the midst of many trials. He is a *bosbia!* His life has inspired believers for thousands of years. But he is very human and can easily be criticized and denigrated, because we all know his story. The paradox is that his spiritual son comes from Bathsheba, with whom he had this illicit affair. Solomon becomes a man of faith who completes the temple of God and fulfills God's promises to Israel.

Our wrongs do not negate what we do right! David is still a hero of the faith and portrayed as a person that can inspire us to seek God and walk according to God's purposes. He was a man who loved God with his whole heart and inspires us to also love God. He was a sinner who needed redemption, not a saint without blemish. All of us have short comings, but if we confess our sins and align our hearts with God, we are credible as Christian heroes. Today we are denigrating our heroes because of their shortcomings, but a Kingdom of grace does not look for moral perfection in anyone except for Christ.

Are you overcoming the negative messages sent by the sin in your life? Have you withdrawn from your call because of shame and guilt? Do you know that ultimately life is not about you, but about Christ in you, the hope of glory and honor?

# 5

## BIBLICAL OR POLITICAL?: SOCIAL JUSTICE AND THE EVANGELICAL DILEMMA

I WILL NOW REFERENCE social injustices and their history. In American history, racism represents injustice and the dominance of one group over another. The history of people using and abusing others for their own benefit is the history of the human race as well as American history.

For some believers, the term "social justice" has a negative connotation. However, for most of us in America, we have been singing Christmas hymns for years that remind us that the Church was not always divided. In the song "O Holy Night," which was written before the great church split of the last century, a whole gospel was represented by the Church. Love and justice were a part of the Kingdom of God and not outside of the faith for anyone who believes in Christ. In 1843 this poem, yet to become a song, had this verse in it:

> Truly He taught us to love one another
> His law is love and His gospel is peace

Chains shall He break for the slave is our brother
And in His name all oppression shall cease

The issues of grace and justice were not divided. The slave was our brother and we were called to love him and set him free from slavery. Social justice was a part of love and grace that was to be given by our Savior as a task to His Church.

The abuses of slavery were well-documented in American history and fought by people of faith like the abolitionists. The book *Uncle Tom's Cabin* was written to expose the atrocities of slavery and give a contextual understanding of injustice in America. It was a challenge for believers to see His Kingdom come and His will being done on earth as it is in heaven, where "all oppression shall cease."

After the Civil War and the abolition of slavery in America, exploitation and abuse did not stop. The abusive labor practices were continued through the Jim Crow caste systems created to maintain racial inequities. The labor system went from slavery to indentured servitude by having African Americans become share-croppers, rather than allowing them to own their own farms. The reparations of slavery were to be that every slave was to be given forty acres and a mule. This concept followed the Old Testament concept for the release of slaves—that they were to be given the resources to achieve financial independence. Unfortunately, in America, this was an unfulfilled promise. The atrocities and false promises were known by many. Howard, who was mentioned earlier, was named the Moses of the Civil War, but failed at his task to integrate slaves into society because the embeddedness of prejudice was nearly impossible to uproot.

Many years later, six million blacks fled the South to escape the consequences of these injustices. This was the greatest migration in the history of America. With that history came many stories of racial abuse. In the book, *The Warmth of Other Suns,*

Isabel Wilkerson writes of the reasons why blacks left the South. She documents the lynchings of Southern history. "Across the South, someone was hanged or burned alive every four days, from 1889 to 1929,"[22] The abuses demonstrated the evil manifest in humanity. It is too easy to overlook our own depravity in the face of such injustices.

In his book, *The Road to Character*, David Brooks tells of A. Phillip Randolph, Bayard Rustin, and Martin Luther King Jr. in their fight against racism in America. They were significant leaders in confronting the evils of racism in America in the last century. These leaders of the Civil Rights Movement led non-violent protests to change the social structure. They knew that, to create a more just society, they had to suffer injustice to bring about justice or a more righteous society. Brooks tells how they first had to develop character and self-control to become leaders successfully fighting systemic evil or social injustice. They first had to be aware of their own personal depravity and face the evils ˙lurking inside themselves:

> Even people on the righteous side of a cause can be corrupted by their own righteousness, can turn a selfless movement into an instrument to serve their own vanity. They can be corrupted by what-ever power they attain and corrupted by their own powerlessness.[23]

Even though the protests focused on injustices found in others, racism could only be overcome with the godly character of those who refused to trade evil for evil, who were willing to face their own sin and have a disciplined godly approach like Jesus. Fighting

---

22   Isabel Wilkerson, *The Warmth of Other Suns: The Epic Story of America's Great Migration* (Vintage Books, 2010), 39.

23   David Brooks, *The Road to Character* (Random House, 2015), 146.

systems that steal human dignity is right and opposing injustice a righteous act, but ignoring one's own sinfulness only perpetuates evil and creates a new system of evil. Can we fight evil both personally *and* socially? Isn't that the call of God for a believer in Christ? Why is this a dilemma for evangelicals?

Soon after the church split between conservatives and liberals in the early 1900's, pietism in the fundamentalist (or soon to become evangelical) Church put such a strong emphasis on personal transformation that social transformation was ignored as a call of God. It was like parts of the Bible were removed and thrown out. The Church almost vilified social transformation, or what had come to be known in this church split as the "social gospel." In one of the churches I worked in, a church leader told me that "good deeds" are a part of the social gospel and said I was pushing heresy and adding to the gospel. I was surprised at his passion and how he could overlook that faith had to be partnered with good deeds to be a true faith.

## SYSTEMIC EVIL—SINS OF IGNORANCE

How is evil established systemically? I believe that without God, many sins are normalized as "just the way we do business." Rationalization is part of being human and fallen. This holds true in the business world, family, politics, church, or any of the domains of social relationships. We all start out with enmeshments and loyalties that are apart from God and His will and Kingdom. Mott comments on this by saying,

> We are socialized into the acceptance or the avoidance of major ethical issues. Our socialization reflects the moral conscience of others who share our position in society, and our ethical reasoning

is shaped before we actually come to reflect upon life or make conscious moral decisions.[24]

This has to do with the development of the individual as well as the social system. The slum-lord, who does his business by exploiting his tenants, justifies and normalizes his business practices. The stepfather who molests his stepchildren may have been molested himself and thus normalizes his behavior. The politician who slanders his opponent justifies his judgments because this is the way everyone runs their race. Bob, in our opening counseling story, hung out with guys who treated women with disrespect and fellowshipped with alcohol. Julie's best friend encouraged her to have an affair, because she felt she was justified by the way that Bob was mistreating her, saying, "Everyone deserves to be loved." All these systems tend to "normalize" things that are unhealthy or sinful for those involved in these systems. As a believer faces himself or herself, they are regenerated by the Holy Spirit and able to help others grow and develop morally and spiritually.

For the believer who is called to transformational work, loyalty to a social domain cannot be higher than loyalty to Christ and His Kingdom, although that does not mean that a Christian should separate from the domains that they are called to serve. Often to become successful and credible in a domain, a person has to become competent in the system and establish themselves. That also can be a faith journey. But if they are more dependent on the domain for their security, significance, and support, it will be difficult to be transformational within that social system. A believer has to have individuation: the ability to stand alone while maintaining connections—not enmeshed in the social system—based on their faith in God. He empowers them to make a difference. The Lord is the one who can facilitate that strength as we grow in our relationship with Him. He does the heart surgery dealing

---

24    Mott, 13.

with our unhealthy connections, dependencies and sinfulness. As we turn to Him He orders the priorities of our loyalties as well. He can strengthen our moral convictions. If we look at Jesus, how He valued God the Father above His loyalty to family, the religious system, or even His disciples, we can see how He was truly radical and transformational. In Christ's teaching He makes plain the cost of discipleship, He says,

> If you want to be my follower you must love me more than your own father and mother, wife and children, brothers and sisters—yes more than your own life. Otherwise, you cannot be my disciple. And you cannot be my disciple if you do not carry your own cross and follow me (Luke 14:25–27).

The highest loyalties, even family and self, are clearly to take a back seat to our loyalty to Christ. If we are to be His disciples, we must be committed to His Kingdom and its transformation of this world. Of course the ambiguity and paradoxes are that, at times, God may have us focus on sacrificial service to family or business or even a godly care for ourselves.

## SOCIAL JUSTICE & INEQUITIES

Social justice is a very complicated issue that goes way beyond the scope of this book, but I want to address some of its simpler aspects. Part of the opening definitions of justice had to do with the "distribution of burdens and benefits" in any social system. When someone gets most of the benefits, while others have most of the burden, the system is an unjust system. However, do most people care how the system affects others? Do they even know or are they consciously aware? Do they care how their attitudes, choices and behaviors affect others? Are they willing to be loving or make the needed changes? Do they even know the stories of the social systems they are connected to within their own lives?

I have seen a lack of reciprocity in marriage and family, businesses, countries, churches, and most social structures. This is often because justice in relationship to equity is overlooked. When I ran a counseling agency, I published a profit and loss statement every month so all employees could see how their efforts were being rewarded. I was attempting to help create a sense of justice and equity. However, I had employees that felt everyone should get the same pay, even if their education levels were not equivalent. The high school graduate wanted to earn the same as the person with a graduate degree. I felt this would not reward those who made greater sacrifices and had taken more risks. It is extremely difficult to have everyone feel that life is fair, and perhaps only God can make life fair and just when He rewards us in the afterlife. Fairness is often a subjective perspective, emotionally based, and often emotionally manipulative. True objectivity in the area of justice and equity is so complex, with so many factors contributing to it. There still needs to be effort put into reciprocity in order to work at justice.

Justice in social systems is based on the mutuality of reciprocity. Good will and positive exchanges occur as long as there is give and take in a relational system. As was stated earlier, Boszormenyi-Nagy says, "reciprocity is defined as mutuality of benefits or gratifications."[25] When there is no reciprocity in relationships, people get angry and withdraw. Relationships are destabilized. Injustice deprives people of the rewards that should be rightfully theirs. Injustice also establishes and supports deprivations and facilitates people being stuck in a life of poverty. That poverty can be a lack of finances, respect, education, power, position, and so many other benefits that can be withheld by those who have these things.

25  Boszormenyi-Nagy, 56.

People who are deeply wounded and embittered may stay negatively entitled because of hurt and injustice. Their part is to forgive, take responsibility, and grow into mature, godly people; otherwise, they will become a part of injustice toward others. I worked with the homeless for many years. So many of them have been abused and neglected. Some are self-absorbed and traumatized. I have often seen them trade evil for good because of their pain, resentment, and fear. Their abuse forms judgments and they then vilify others and are limited in their ability to love well. Those who help them often quit because of the lack of reciprocity and the experience of giving good and getting abused in the process. On the other hand, I have experienced many homeless people who are very appreciative and more than reciprocate by being thankful and working hard, and who are kind to those who care.

## NEW TESTAMENT EQUITY

When Paul talks about giving in the book of Corinthians, he uses the theme of equity. He does not want some to be overly burdened and others to have it too easy. "For this is not for the ease of others and for your affliction, but by way of equality" (2 Corinthians 8:13). The "haves" are not vilified in comparison to the "have-nots." He also addresses reciprocity in verse fourteen when he says, "Right now you have plenty and can help them. Then at some other time they can share with you when you need it. In this way everyone's needs will be met" (2 Corinthians 8:14). He cares about reciprocity and circularity. However, giving in these passages is not based on the motivation of reciprocity, but on the spiritual. The focus is a person's walk with God—that God's will is for us to be generous and that He will provide for us and reward our giving. "Don't give reluctantly or in response to pressure. For God loves the person who gives cheerfully. And God will generously provide all you need" (2 Corinthians 9:7–8). The spiritual is not meant to minimize the horizontal relationships, but to undergird the justice aspects of human relationships. The relationship with God grants a grace that is often essential for justice to be established. Often, sacrifice is required by those who have or possess. Fear holds an unjust exchange in place. Without God's provision and promises to be just and gracious, people are more often governed by fear than generosity or faith.

Jesus was able to be sacrificial because He trusted God; therefore, He did what was right and just according to God's will and was not limited by the sins of others. So, He suffered, but with the assurance that God would make the wrongs right.

> This suffering is all part of what God has called you to. Christ, who suffered for you, is your example. Follow in his steps. He never sinned, and he never deceived anyone. He did not retaliate when he was insulted. When he suffered, he did not threaten to get even. He left his case in the hands of God, who always judges fairly (1 Peter 2:21–23).

So justice is established by trusting in a God who judges rightly and helps us, through faith, to do the right thing rather than the wrong.

****

Although we cannot govern when blessings will come to us, God promises to be faithful and provide. I went through a divorce about fifteen years into the ministry. I had worked too hard, married young and neglected my marriage. When my wife left me, I resigned as pastor of the church that I started with another man named Jim Olson. I was ashamed and broken in my marriage failure. Part of my disillusionment was that I had been bi-vocational for the first ten years of being a pastor, so the amount of sacri-fice made this trial feel so unfair. I was hurt, angry and alienated. I felt like all the work, faith, sacrifice and suffering was in vain. This was a time of deep reflection, of wondering if this was worth it. I sold my business five years before I resigned as a pastor. In six years I had doubled its value, plus got a ten-year mortgage on the property at 9%.

When I resigned from the church, all the property was free and clear and had increased in value many fold, yet I was given a month's severance pay. The new pastor had a full salary and bene-fits and the property was debt free. My disillusionment centered around thinking, *Was it worth investing my life in God's Kingdom and in other people's lives? If I make sacrifices and am treated with disdain, should I still trust in God and be obedient?*

The same held true when I reflected on my marriage. *Years of working hard so my wife could stay at home and be a mother to my children, and divorce was my reward?* The sacrifice and effort was definitely being called into question and my human side was alive and well. My devotion to God and living for His glory was now more than ever being called into question! *Where was God and His faithfulness?*

One of the men I had discipled years before called me. He had gone into business and was doing well, working for Morgan-Stanley in Chicago. He had become a "have" and I was very conscious of being a "have-not." I had lost so much in my failure: home, position, career, dignity, family, money, and many of my dreams. Al asked if I wanted to fly to Hilton Head, South Carolina and learn to play golf. I replied that golf was for old people. I was depressed and grieving. I wasn't used to being on the receiving end of the line. He was going to pay for it all. He asked me to pray about it. I had been the giver and I wasn't sure I could humbly receive, after all I did not deserve this grace.

The next week he called and said he had prayed about it and he had bought me a round-trip ticket to fly me there. I had invested in Al and he had even worked for me in a business I ran, a self-service car wash. I did not expect he would be the person to reciprocate in my hour of need. I had invested in men who became pastors, missionaries, and church and para-church leaders, and I did not hear from them in my time of feeling marginalized. At the end of a great week in Hilton Head, Al Mueller came to me and handed me a check for a significant amount of money and basically said, "God isn't discarding you. You have a future in Him."

I was considering starting a non-profit counseling agency, but my question became, *Should I start a for-profit business instead? Would that give me more control over my life? Maybe I would be less vulnerable?* I was deeply moved by Al's generosity and kindness. It was a hand up in a time of feeling like I had fallen a long way down. A businessman had manifested the grace of God in my life and I did not see this coming. This simple act of kindness helped stabilize my faith in God.

I discovered during this time another layer of sin and pride. As a young man I had learned that, with a little effort and focus I could climb the hill to success faster than most, and standing on that hilltop made me feel important and significant. A few years prior to my fall I had a denominational leader court me, saying, "Your church is the best church I have seen in America." Now, I was a sidelined pastor who had failed.

This breaking revealed my self-centeredness and self-righteousness, which put me more in touch with my humanity and encouraged me to share more of my brokenness. *How often do others feel disillusioned in their faith?* We are all called to live for Christ and not ourselves, but this struggle is pretty universal (2 Corinthians 5:14–15). Being able to relate to others' struggles with faith made me more empathetic and human. I love the quote by a popular psychiatrist who says, "I never met a client I could not identify with." He must be a little crazy!

Being broken after working so hard in my faith granted me a view of grace that was deeper than I'd had before. I was humbled by the grace of God shown through Al and others during this time. I was not special or significant because of achievement. I had failed, but I felt loved and cared for. My brokenness leveled the playing field and I was starting over with little to show for it. I didn't even have a home to offer anyone who would be interested in me. A few years later, Ted Bednar, a builder and a single dad in my church, built me a beautiful home for his cost so I could afford to start over. Without the kindness and generosity of these gracious men, I would not have had the resources to put my life and faith back together. I also realized that people who lasted in ministry were a little more selfish, because they were willing to receive.

## FROM INEQUITY TO EQUITY

Some have said that the ground is level at the foot of the cross. Paul says, "There is no longer Jew or Gentle, slave or free, male or female" (Galatians 3:28). The gospel sought to eliminate divisions that were oppressive and to empower us to love one another. In our country, there has been a lack of equity in how people are valued. Slaves and females did not have the same rights or value as others. When voting rights were given, both women and blacks were only given three fifths the rights of a human being. Full voting rights did not come until much later in American history. What most people do not know is that poor whites and indentured servants also could not vote. It was not just gender or skin color that marginalized people, but also socioeconomic status. Those lacking development and resources were seen as inferior, a judgment that created a prejudice that perpetuated an inferior

status for many in our culture. So many were never given opportunities to develop because it was assumed they were just inferior.

What was ignored was the fact that many in these categories
could grow and become amazing people. For example, George
Washington Carver was born a slave and became one of America's
most brilliant soil scientists and an amazing Christian man. George
almost single-handedly saved the South when they had depleted
the soil through cotton farming. He introduced peanuts as a crop
that replenished the soil and allowed farming to prosper again.
He spent much of his life learning and becoming educated far
beyond the average professor—and yet, he was born a slave. He
grew and developed through faith, education, and service at a
time when racism often denied the possibility of development
and potential. Perhaps his greatest character trait was perseverance. In the book about his life, *George Washington Carver—The
Man Who Overcame* by Lawrence Elliott, Carver does, like many
of the poor, get discouraged and gives up hope of getting into
college. However, he does find encouraging people that help him
try again to gain a college education and he succeeds.

Because of judgments held by those with different socioeconomic status, opportunities to grow and develop were often denied
for those of a lesser status or position. Resistance or road blocks
often cause people who already feel powerless to give up and stop
trying to improve their lives. That did not stop people like George
Washington Carver, who left his family at a young age and worked
hard so he could go to school in another town. Often people find
value and the motivation through their faith to gain personal
visions to better themselves. They may also gain the courage to
fight oppression, and then find the freedom to have better lives.

# 6

## REWARDS:
## THE INEQUITY OF GRACE

T HERE SEEMS, AT TIMES, to be inequity in the Scriptures. In Matthew 20:1–16, an estate owner hires people to work in his Vineyard throughout the day but pays them all the same wage. Some feel that they have been treated unfairly and protest their payment. Jesus teaches this story and it tells the story of grace, getting what we don't deserve. He paid the price for our salvation—we did not earn it. Justice, on the other hand, is getting what we do deserve. The thief on the cross next to Jesus is invited into paradise by Jesus and does not earn his way into heaven but is granted grace. There will be many people in heaven who most of us will be surprised to see. Many people struggle with grace, even religious people who feel that, because of their righteousness, they are better than others and therefore should be afforded a greater reward. The reward of salvation is a relationship with God for all eternity, which is the greatest grace we could ever be given. However, salvation is a gift not based on merit, so it seems unfair to many. Justice and grace seem at times incompatible, but the Kingdom is based on grace. Justice, especially punitive justice, has been taken care of by Christ, who paid our debt because he loves us. Yesterday, I spoke with a man and his wife who borrowed $7,000 from a title loan company. He has been making payments for three years and still owes $6,500. Without grace, he will never pay off his debt—someone will have to help him. We are helping him with his debt because we care about him, his wife and child, because Jesus cares. Jesus paid off the debt we could not afford to pay off and that was grace. What brings equity to the sacrifice and work of our lives is that our efforts are rewarded.

## SOCIAL JUSTICE, EQUITY, AND EMPOWERMENT THROUGH BIBLICAL REWARDS

The Bible seems to discuss three main rewards relating to our work. The first is that *a just wage* is expected because those who work deserve their pay (Luke 10:7). In the movie *Something the Lord Made*, Vivien Thomas struggles with being an unedu-cated black man, working with Dr. Alfred Blalock, a prominent surgeon. All three of the areas of reward are addressed in this movie. The issue of a just wage is addressed when Vivien cannot make a living wage as a medical assistant because he is given a lower position as a maintenance worker at the hospital. He is deprived of the financial resources that should be given to him in a world that does not have righteousness as a goal. This injus-tice is corrected as he stands up for himself, finds his voice, and asks for a just wage.

*Honor* is the second reward from Scripture. "And give respect and honor to whom it is due" (Romans 13:7b). Vivien and Alfred work together to make medical history by discovering how to reverse traumatic shock and are also the first in the world to do heart surgery. When the successful surgery is performed, Dr. Blalock is skyrocketed into a position of honor and glory as a pioneer in the field of medicine, although it is Vivien Thomas who had taught Dr. Blalock how to do the surgery. He is ignored and excluded from a place of honor because he is black and has no degree. In God's economy, everything is to be stewarded according to God's will, even honor. Vivien quits working for Dr. Blalock because of the offenses of this slight: feeling disrespected, exploited, and excluded. He says he and his contributions are invisible to the world, but is hurt because Dr. Blalock overlooks the recognition that he deserves. Vivien's dream was to be a medical doctor. He does not get the chance to go to school because of a bank collapse and then, after fifteen years of working with the very best in medicine, he is not given any academic credit for his life experience and ends up selling antacids. The educational system's credibility is granted through deductive learning from books, rather than inductive learning through experience and life contexts. So, he experiences almost no positional empowerment because of the rigidity of the academic and medical systems he has so faithfully served. They have benefited from his hard work, intelligence, competence, and innovation, while he has been overlooked—a grave injustice.

The last of the three rewards I will call *glory*, which I will define as a position of prominence or esteem. "He will give eternal life to those who persist in doing what is good, seeking after the glory and honor and immortality that God offers" (Romans 2:7). "And when Christ who is your real life is revealed to the whole world, you will share in all his glory" (Colossians 3:4). At the end of the movie, Vivien Thomas is given an honorary doctorate and his portrait is hung in the lobby of Johns Hopkins Hospital. This is more about the substance of Vivien's life, in that he did great work and was on a great mission, but also that he ended up seeing some justice towards the end of his life. Like an athlete who wins a gold medal and shines in the light of this glory, Vivien is given glory.

This is a great story based on real-life events about the issues of race and justice in the context of great contribution in the medical field. It is told from the perspective of Vivien Thomas to give us a view of what it was like to be a black man in his position. It is done well in that there is ambiguity in the story. Dr. Blalock is absorbed in his call and mission to make a difference in the medical field and, like many mission-driven people, he falls short in loving others well, which is portrayed with his family as well as Vivien. Dr. Blalock is a wealthy, white doctor of high position who is insensitive to Vivien's humble position and the injustice issues that are experienced by Vivien, a black man without position or status. Dr. Blalock does give Vivien a position of significance through sharing his work with him, which Vivien acknowledges is an honor. The movie also tells about Alfred Blalock's loyalty to Vivien and how that costs him in an age of racism, so there is an acknowledgment of grace in the midst of sin, arrogance, and insensitivity.

Dr. Blalock is powerless in the face of systemic injustice. Vivien is not allowed to come in the front entrance of John's Hopkins Hospital. Even though there is a statue of Jesus with open arms, and even with Blalock's high position as chief of surgery, he cannot have Vivien come with him through the front door. All lower-status workers, including Vivien, can only enter through the rear entrance. The paradox and ambiguity of the situation is that this prestigious institution has adopted the Kingdom *mission* to heal through modern medicine, but not the Kingdom *value* of dignity for all people. Here is an institution that partially submits to the King but ignores other requirements of the Kingdom. Even though the system lacks godliness, Dr. Blalock and Vivien find a taste of the Kingdom in their work. In their work partnership,

Vivien does heart surgery on dogs, and Dr. Blalock admires Vivien's work so much that the title of the movie comes from a compliment given by Dr. Blalock who says that Vivien's sutures are, "Like something the Lord made." They are almost perfect! There are wonderful moments of partnership, humility, and validation of Vivien's talent and intelligence by Dr. Blalock. So even though the story is told through the eyes of an African American who experiences tremendous lack of basic benefits for his work—which equals injustice—it is told with fairness and grace.

## CONTRACTS

Another part of the complexity of justice is contracts. If a person agrees to work for minimum wage, that is a contract. Social justice considers contracts as binding. A person who steps into a contract with a title loan company is held accountable, even though in my opinion the interest rate of 204% is immoral or unjust. The court system considers contracts as binding. I worked with a woman who took out a payday loan at 1,000%, defaulted on the loan, and lost in court. The judgment went against her because of the contract. Desperate people often will accept contracts that are not good for them.

In the 1980's, I did a lot of work with families in which people were abused. Many of the women accepted abusive men into their lives because they paid the bills and had more power and they needed help. Over a period of time, this abuse or injustice brought a change in the contract because the pain was too much. The equation of burdens to blessings was gone and the burden became overwhelming. One woman I worked with said her alcoholic husband beat her almost every week. I asked why she put up with this abuse and she said, "I was afraid I would lose him." She was very insecure and he provided some security.

Poor individuation and a belief that things would be worse if she changed kept her stuck. Eventually, she felt more anxious over having him in her life than being without him.

I had a pastor whose wife was physically abusing him as he battled cancer, but he was embarrassed and so failed to set a boundary with her. Most social situations have ambiguity, a combination of good with the bad. Vivien said, "I like the work." However, he was unjustly treated and not paid enough, but was valued for his skill and given opportunities that brought honor. In mature relationships people take responsibility for their decisions and social contracts, but can renegotiate a bad contract. That maturity may take years to develop. Sometimes there is not much of a choice and, whether in work or family contracts, people are abused and accept it. The "worth it" question is always a part of the contract evaluation on every one's part. Is Vivien's pay enough? Is he valuable to Dr. Blalock?

## REWARDS

Since rewards seem to be a big part of the discussion on justice, they cannot be ignored. Benefits for our efforts are part of the definition of justice. However, many believers would say that they do not seek rewards but just want to do what is right! That is a mark of maturity and character, because it takes time and paying a price before rewards come our way. Rewards are really too complex a subject to cover in a small section of a book about justice but I will do my best to summarize.

There are so many contexts to acknowledge that grant us a just and rewarding life. For example, when the man I mentioned gets his debt paid off and has financial freedom it will be a reward for those of us working to see him free from this oppressive loan. Most of the Bible has conditional promises, and with those promises come blessings and rewards, or curses and punishments. A lot of my writing on the Psalms covers these rewards or blessings, which come from walking in faith and experiencing our good deeds or good works being rewarded. They also cover sin and bringing negative consequences on ourselves, like David acknowledges in his story. When people make commitments, do the right things, and work hard, God blesses them in the context of difficulty.

Also Jesus, when addressing His Kingdom, says plainly that He will reward believers for doing His will. "See, I am coming soon, and my reward is with me, to repay all according to their deeds" (Revelation 22:12). There will not be any sacrifice, suffering, or service that goes unrecognized or unrewarded in the Kingdom of Heaven. There are "no little people or little places" as Dr. Schaeffer used to say. God is just, but also gracious in His dealings with us.

\*\*\*\*

I have many friends in my congregation and community that have inspired me with their lives. I have watched them work hard, struggle, and be rewarded for their accomplishments over the years. I lived in community with Scott and Jenny Edminster when I was a young pastor. Scott was in medical school and they were starting a family—heroic tasks. Fighting disease is fighting evil and each domain that is entered will have its own definition of evil. Scott and Jenny partnered together in the domain of medicine and family. Scott has quite a story, but I will just hit some highlights.

Scott worked in a hospital as an ER doctor, where he developed relationships with doctors in other specialties. He decided that God was calling him to start a free clinic for the gap group, the working poor who were underinsured and uninsured. He called it Christ Clinic, and it was run mainly through volunteer doctors. Scott was recognized as "Spokane County Physician Citizen of the Year" for his philanthropic work with those who needed medical resources and could not afford them. God blessed him in his efforts and rewarded his accomplishments.

One of the high values in the Kingdom of God is productivity. We are not to bury our talents but use them to glorify God and bless others. Jesus makes this clear in the story of the noble man who assigns service to ten servants in Luke 19:11–27. There are great rewards for the two who increased what was given them and chastisement for the one who did not produce and the ones who ignored the call to service. Scott is one of many leaders that God has granted temporal rewards. He and Jenny have five children. They are very proud of their children and have seen many rewards for their parental calling. They have complimented each other in their roles. Scott says Jenny was the "kind one" and not the "mean" one. I have seen fathers and mothers work together in different roles, where the men focus on requiring tasks of the children to be done well. They often come across as demanding, where the mothers focus on the nurture and believing the best, coming across as the accepting ones. They are not mutually exclusive but often complimentary, especially when they respect each other. Children are a reward from God (Psalm 127:3), especially those that honor their parents and cause them to feel proud rather than ashamed. Rewards are also related to life tasks and how we invest in those life tasks. Both Scott and Jenny have taken on many life tasks using their talents to do God's will, and have rewards from their efforts. Rewards are contextual and that is why heaven will be so amazing.

Rewards are so significant in life. Why do we do what we do? Why do we invest in what we invest in? What is really valuable in life? Do we believe that God is a rewarder of those that diligently seek Him and do His will? Everyone loves winning and loves a winner—just look at all the movies about victory and professional sports. What means the most to you? Having our families proud of us is a reward for so many of us. What about those who do not have families who believe in them? So many defer rewards in the moment for rewards that will only come in the future. Do we believe we have an eternal future that we can invest our lives in? Having God proud of us, saying, "Well done good and faithful servant," may be the greatest reward we can experience.

The rewards of the Kingdom of God are different than the rewards of the world and yet many times the same, because God blesses us here. A nice house, successful career, good family—all of these can be rewards from God and part of His will. They also can be distractions from truly knowing and serving God. Only God knows a person's heart and the motives of their heart. To transition into heavenly rewards rather than just worldly rewards is a part of the journey of faith.

> Don't store up treasures here on earth, where moths eat them and rust destroys them, and where thieves break in and steal. Store your treasures in heaven, where moths and rust cannot destroy, and thieves do not break in and steal. Wherever your treasure is there the desires of your heart will also be (Matthew 6:19–21).

\*\*\*\*

There is a verse that validates differences of expression. "So whether you eat or drink, or whatever you do, do it all for the glory of God" (1 Corinthians 10:31). We have many gifts and can use them to glorify God and benefit others.

Patti Triplett, who did the painting for the cover of this book, is an artist. Beauty is a way of fighting the evil and ugliness of life and is used by many artists to bring glory to God for His creation. Patti is very gifted, as you can see, and does beautiful work. She loves to do her artwork and finds herself in this expression. Patti is also a mother who has raised 3 boys. She partnered with Ed, her husband, to do a great job raising her sons. All of her contributions in life bring glory to God and will not be forgotten. There is no "sacred versus secular" in the Kingdom of God because we all have different gifts and express our faith in different contexts. Whether a doctor or an artist, a mother or a father, all our roles and gifts can be used for the common good and will be rewarded by God.

## REWARDS ARE CONTEXTUAL

For most people, rewards are accomplishing their purposes. For the businessman, making a profit is at least one of the purposes in the domain of business, and prosperity a promise of God. For a mother, raising healthy and independent children is one of the rewards of her efforts, and another promise of God's Word. For a policeman, catching bad guys is one of the rewards of the job. This is about retributive justice, holding people accountable for their crimes.

One of the men in our church was an intensely devoted policeman. His name is Robbie Mayer. He caught a man who was terrorizing our community, who was called the "Primetime Rapist" because he would enter houses usually during the 6 o'clock news to rob and rape the occupants. There was such a sense of threat and dread that home protection businesses were booming. The community of Tucson was vibrating with anxiety and it needed deliverance. One of the goals of Robbie was to catch "bad men" and take them off the streets so our community would be a safe place to live, and he did this well. We desperately needed peace and the alleviation of threat and trauma. That is also a call of God, and peace and safety are a part of His blessings. Robbie's call and purpose was to hold people accountable who were breaking the law and victimizing innocent people. Robbie prayed and believed that God "reveals secrets" and as he did his detective work, he believed God would lead him to those predators. I have known Robbie for many years and have been inspired by his dedication and success in finding horrible criminals that have to be taken out of society to make it safe for others. A few years after the "Primetime Rapist" was no longer a threat, most people took the bars off their windows because Robbie and others had made the community safe.

## CALLINGS ARE CONTEXTUAL

Callings and rewards are contextual. The primary context for the believers is their relationship with God. Are they responding to the Spirit of God? Do they know God's Word and trust and obey His Truth? Do they harden their hearts when God speaks to them or surrender to His will? Only God can truly answer that question. No one can judge our callings or the context of our calling because God is personal, speaking to each person in the context of their own life. Today many are judging people of the past and disqualifying them because of the morals and values of the present. Our context was not their context. Was George Washington a hero because of his courage and godliness or a bad man because he had slaves? Was he worthy or our admiration and honor or was he to be denigrated because of his shortcomings?

There was a book and movie about a hero of World War II named Desmond Doss. He did not believe that he should carry a gun, but wanted to be a soldier. The men in his unit judged him as a coward and a rebel. He signed up to be a medic so he could give life and not take life. He believed God had called him to this role and position. He did not believe that everyone was called to be a medic, but he was. He was a man of great faith and carried his Bible with him into battle. He read Psalm 91 and believed God's promises were given for his safety. When he escaped death and succeeded in his missions, the stories of his faith went out to troops all over the world. He received the Congressional Medal of Honor, the only conscientious objector (CO) to receive this award.

As I was reading a book about his life, I came across a passage in the book of Hebrews that says that all people of vital faith need heroes—people who inspire us to be better people. "Then you will not become spiritually dull and indifferent. Instead, you will follow the example of those who are going to inherit God's promises because of their faith and patience" (Hebrews 6:11–12). The passage then cites Abraham as an example for us to emulate. There are many inspirational heroes who challenge us to courage, faith, hard work, and patience for results. All of us need heroes like Desmond Doss or others who inspire us. Yet we can dismiss heroes by being judgmental.

\*\*\*\*

In complex systems, there are many roles that need to be played and many purposes that may oppose another person's purpose. A prosecuting attorney opposes a defense attorney because they have different purposes—one to protect a person's rights and the other to hold a person accountable for their wrongs.

I was a board member for a housing ministry. The mission was to be a safety net and provide housing for those facing homelessness and to do restorative justice in the context of recovery. We wanted to be a community development corporation with cooperation from people with different purposes. We had the police on campus and several organizations that did recovery work. The conflict over different purposes constantly created friction and lawsuits. I was seeing policemen in counseling who only heard the "bad stories" of people breaking laws and had not heard the good stories—very different narratives. People form their opinions by the stories they listen to, and contradictory stories are often hard to process once value judgments are formed and supported by their group.

We had a woman there that was to be sentenced to prison for drug use, but the judge ordered her to stay at our ministry called In n Up. She got sober, finished her education, became a Christian, and worked to earn a Masters degree in Social Work, then took a job at the VA hospital. Almost all the police who I told this story to could not believe this story of transformation. It was true! It just contradicted the stories they had heard about law breakers. The woman's brother-in-law, a corporate attorney, was so impressed by her progress that he represented us for free in our lawsuits.

Retributive justice and restorative justice often seem opposed to each other, in purpose. The question often becomes, what are the positive benefits or rewards that come from different roles, gifts and outcomes? Can we see them, or are we too self-centered to acknowledge that God may work to accomplish His purposes in the complexity of our world?

\*\*\*\*

There are so many different callings and many that seem to be at cross purposes to one another, so acceptance is primary in the Kingdom of God. We are to do God's will God's way. These issues are so complex and over simplifying them even creates problems. When Paul in Romans addresses different approaches to life, he warns us to not be judgmental. Missions or callings often cause us to be at cross purposes and create values conflicts: *this is good and that is bad,* or even, *I'm good and you are bad,* over simplifying often complex issues. Paul says,

Accept Christians who are weak in faith, and don't argue with them about what they think is right or wrong.... They are responsible to the Lord, so let him tell them whether they are right or wrong. The Lord's power will help them do as they should (Romans 14:1, 4).

We all get to our callings and convictions from many different contexts. God grants us freedom to be individuals! Knowing God's will for ourselves does not mean we know God's will for everyone else, especially in the areas of conscience and faith.

One of my friends and pastoral colleagues, who I have mentioned before, Jerry Peyton, has a passion for protecting people from predators. He started and ran an organization called Sold No More, which dealt with sex trafficking. There are so many terrible stories in this area of injustice that lately it has been very engaging for many believers who hear His call. Jerry was instrumental in doing preventative work in the school systems as well as crisis interventions with unjust laws which did not protect underage girls from being prostituted by sex predators. Sold No More has been recognized nationally and adopted by school systems across the nation. The injustices of abuse create the passion for protection and Jerry has seen success in his work. He has an amazing legacy. Jerry has a passion to create safety, just like Robbie, and both are needed for safety to be established and maintained in our community.

Our God is much bigger than our personal worlds or missions, and so are our differences. We need people doing preventative work *and* crisis interventions to have safe communities. Prevention may focus on the prevention of evil, where crisis intervention may have to be inclusive of those struggling with evil. The values may clash.

I have other friends who focus on inclusion and do not want others to feel unloved. Many of the missional people I know who work in recovery, homelessness, or with ex-offenders see those who have missions of protection—like Jerry or Robbie—as excluding those who need the most help. Libby Wright, who was homeless at one time almost always would take in homeless people when I could not find a place for them to stay. Larry Munguia who runs the S.O.B.E.R. Project would embrace those struggling with addiction. God is a big God with multiple purposes and He values all of our callings.

> For the Kingdom of God is not a matter of what you eat or drink, but of living a life of goodness, and peace, and joy in the Holy Spirit. If you serve Christ with this attitude, you will please God. And other people will approve of you, too. So then, let us aim for harmony in the church and try to build each other up (Romans 14:17–19).

# 7

## WE ARE NOT ALL THE SAME:
## INEQUITY AND DIFFERENCES

P ART OF THE COMPLEXITY of inequity has to do with differences. We are not the same and neither are the contexts of our
lives. What may seem to be an inequity may be related to differences that are grounded in context, creation, and God's sovereignty.
This becomes so complex that I will not try to develop the ideas
of inequities because of differences, though they are prominent
in life. It is obvious that the person who is very gifted in intelligence and emotional intelligence will do much better in American
life than the person who is less intelligent, less educated, easily
frustrated, and quits tasks before completing them; so the benefits will vary tremendously. These may appear to be injustices, but
we are not all created equal in giftedness or contextual resources.
There are so many studies now related to what allows people to
succeed or prosper in life and what renders them to failure and
deprivation. Without family stability and education, we see a
much higher rate of poverty. Lack of resources creates inequities,

and is an inequity contextually. Poor health and healthcare are also factors that leave out essential resources for our well-being. I have worked with many who are buried in medical debt, which keeps them from getting ahead. Arizona has some of the worst demographics in the area of education. In several of the southside schools that I have been involved with, the parents are required to sign contracts so the kids will be committed to studying and finishing their high school education. In past years, I have worked with schools that had dropout rates as high as 50%. We know that work, practice, and endurance play major roles in success or prosperity, so endurance is essential to prosperity. What happens to kids whose parents discourage education? High expectations are a resource for direction and vision, and the opposite is also true. Those who suffer well towards achieving their goals do so much better than those who have little perseverance.

In the book *Outliers*, Gladwell talks about how practice is the major factor separating those who master a skill like a musical instrument. He says,

> The thing that distinguishes one performer from another is how hard he or she works. That's it. And what's more, the people at the very top don't just work harder or even much harder than everyone else. They work much, much, much harder. The idea that excellence at performing a complex task requires a critical minimum level of practice surfaces again and again in studies of expertise. In fact, researchers have settled on what they believe is the magic number for true expertise—ten thousand hours.[26]

---

26    Malcolm Gladwell, *Outliers: The Story of Success* (New York: Little, Brown & Co., 2008), 40.

This is where Scripture teaches that faith without works is dead! First comes the thought, idea, or belief, and then comes the action.

Are we practicing our faith? Are we listening to God in the context of our lives and trusting Him and His word? The book of James clearly states that unless we hear God's Word, and then act on it, our faith is dead or useless.

There are amazing heroes of the faith that have conquered kingdoms, as Hebrews chapter eleven states. This is recorded in history with people and nations. William Wilberforce, a national reformer, dedicated his life to bringing in the "goodness of God" to the nation of England when it was full of immorality. He worked extremely hard at it and made tremendous sacrifices to achieve God's calling on His life. This started with a call from God and a work to do, and led to tremendous Kingdom achievement.

Faith calls us to make sacrifices for the greater good, probably the call to sacrifice our lives, whether in terms of time, or in terms of making the greatest sacrifice.

George Washington had the role of a hero—a general—in the Revolutionary War against Britain. He required his soldiers to lay down their lives for future generations. He said to his troops, "We must resolve to conquer or die."[27] Washington led by example and took huge risks personally. He walked in faith believing it was the grace or providence of God that would bring victory. In his call to war with Britain he believed it was about injustice. He believed that America would have to fight, with all the risks involved, to right this wrong. "If I did not think our struggle was just...",[28] Washington says, he would not have taken on the task of war. If this was not a just cause, he makes it clear, he would've

---

27    Ron Chernow, *Washington: A Life.* (London: Penguin Books, 2010), 244.

28    Ibid., 246.

rather been home. He also struggled to develop competencies with his troops so they could win this war and freedom for future generations.

Stages of development, whether from childhood or developing countries, produce different results and rewards. A ten-year-old who has practiced a thousand hours will not have the same rewards or accomplishments as a twenty-year-old who has put in ten thousand hours of practice. Different levels of development produce different rewards. Does that make life unfair or inequitable? The same is true for nations. The ones that work hard on the complex tasks of creating and governing a nation and accomplishing these tasks have more success.

Knowing the tasks and working hard to accomplish them is also essential for success. The Scriptures say,

> Be strong and courageous and do the work. Don't
> be afraid or discouraged by the size of the task, for
> the LORD God, my God, is with you. He will not
> fail you or forsake you (1 Chronicles 29:20).

Gladwell's studies show that almost all competencies are related to hard work and practice. Reward and punishment, or concepts of justice, also come from what we value or reward.

So, what happens when a person does not develop competencies? I am consistently dealing with ex-offenders who were abused and neglected as children and thought that they would not be alive by twenty years of age. Because they have violated the law, they're punished rather than rewarded in their lives. They have very different childhood contexts than those who have resources and are rewarded for their efforts. However, there is a lot of complexity to context. Some develop easily and others struggle because of differences, developmental disabilities, and giftedness. What if, putting in ten thousand hours of practice is not a price they are interested in paying? How does that affect our life and value system? What if parents do not value education because of their culture? Is it right or just to give assistance in an area where people do not want help? Should you make your child practice his clarinet one or two hours a day? I have worked with hundreds of homeless over the years and found that many will never aspire to better positions. Often, they have accepted that they will never get ahead or be blessed. They just do not value or have an orientation for some of the things that middle-class America values.

In one of the homeless shelters I have worked, many of the homeless needed dental care. They had neglected their teeth and lost many of them. I engaged a group of dentists to work on their mouths, pulling teeth, making partials and dentures. The problem was that even after gaining these resources, which made it easier to get jobs and eat, some of them still did not value taking care of their mouths, or have self-care as a personal discipline. The first two I worked with lost their new dentures within one week of getting them. The injustice was that the dentists made sacrifices that were not valued by the homeless, so their efforts were not rewarded.

Many of the people I have worked with are happier with simpler lifestyles, and multitasking is too stressful for them. There are different levels of functioning, stress tolerance, giftedness, energy, and stability that affect a person's level of well-being. The "worth it" question always comes into play on justice issues. *Is it worth working for? Is it valuable enough to work to maintain it? Does the equation of work to reward seem like it is worth it?* Hope and faith play a major part in persevering to receive a blessing. What may appear as an inequity may be a choice of lifestyle. One man's reward is leisure, while another's is a big home. Differences in what we value may or may not reflect injustices.

As therapists, my colleagues and I are required to have treatment plans that are contracts with clients so the therapeutic goals are ethical and not imposing our values and goals on others. Recognizing differences and working with them are a part of forming good therapeutic agreements. That does not mean that we do not define health and pathology to help formulate these treatment goals. An alcoholic who comes in for marital counseling may only want his spouse to be able to handle his drinking and, instead, finds that he has to commit to sobriety to save his marriage. Differences both individually and culturally need to be brought into the equation to understand justice and equity.

There are areas that have tremendous complexity regarding justice and injustice. Today, with multiculturalism, people are often looking for places where they can be accepted, and where they do not have to change to fit a culture, family, or place. The bar may fit the alcoholic, but the marriage may marginalize the alcoholic because his or her behaviors negatively affect the spouse. One of our most basic needs is the need to belong, to be connected, to feel like we are important. Too often, we look for life in all the wrong places. God can offer a place to connect, to belong and to be valued. He also can offer hope and faith in the process and that helps people have a better life.

> So, let's not get tired of doing what is good [working hard towards a goal]. At just the right time we will reap a harvest of blessing if we don't give up (Galatians 6:9).

## CIRCULARITY & INJUSTICE

Circularity has to do with how people affect each other. Being just means sharing the responsibilities and rewards. A victim may be lazy and become a burden to others, but feel entitled not to contribute. A perpetrator or exploiter may selfishly and insensitively dominate others and victimize them through abusing their power. Both of them are contributing to the sickness of a relational system and the sin of each other.

Complexity and circularity help us to see that there is no *them versus us* or *good guys versus bad guys* because of the biblical view that "All have sinned and fall short..." (Romans 3:23). That does not mean that some are not greater sinners than others. Each situation needs to be closely evaluated before we start our definitions of the problem and solutions. Justice is difficult because of sin and selfishness. In linear thinking we tend to look for cause and effect, which may over-simplify the complexities of a matter. *Who is the bad guy causing the injustice and who is the good, innocent victim?* This can be a moral model of black and white thinking, the paradigm of modernity. In systemic thinking we see that, much of the time, everyone contributes to the problem in some way. In postmodernity there is a *multi*-verse rather than a *uni*-verse. There are many stories contributing to the larger story and themes of the problem. However, everyone may also contribute to the solution, so there is a lot more ambiguity in this thinking. Of course, every situation has a context that sets the stage for who is culpable for what, and who helps contribute to the solutions.

## RELATED AND CULPABLE

When I was doing the work to help organize the faith community to eliminate payday loans in our state, I saw some very interesting things. Of the first two hundred evangelicals I talked to about these lending practices in our community, none of them knew that the interest rates were approaching 400% APR, even though these loans were everywhere in our community. When they found out, they were upset and shocked. They just did not know these stories from their own community. I learned that most evangelicals were upwardly mobile and disconnected from the poor of our community. These were sins of ignorance (Luke 23:34). However, as I spoke in churches, I saw new awareness come to many about how these injustices were related to them and the people affected by them.

For example, a Sunday school leader in a Baptist church came to me and said, "I realized after your talk that many of my workers are struggling because they are not making a living wage. I thought they were just financially irresponsible, but as I began to listen to them, I realized they lacked resources. They lacked knowledge and did not know how to stay out of debt, budget, invest, and make their lives work. I have started to help them with no-interest loans. I helped one of them buy his first house, and I now see things I never saw before."

Perhaps his depravity was from ignorance and then from sins of omission. He had to know the story and what God required of him before he could be in right relationship with God and others. To be devout in his faith, he needed to seek God and value Him. That would make him aware of how God feels about the poor being exploited which would then direct his walk of faith.

> He has told you, O man, what is good; and what the LORD requires of you. But to do justice, to love kindness, and to walk humbly with your God (Micah 6:8).

# 8

## LABOR:
## EMPLOYMENT AND
## SOCIAL INJUSTICES

S OCIAL JUSTICE IS CARING about inequities and doing something about them. It is not just the redistribution of wealth
and resources; it is determining who has what and how there can
be more equality.

In the movie, *Same Kind of Different As Me*, Denver Moore,
an African American, tells his story of growing up in Louisiana
as a sharecropper. In this system, "the man," who was a white
man, owned a plantation. It was usually a cotton plantation and
employed "colored folks" to do the work on the land. The compensation was that the employees received a place to live, land to grow
their food, two pigs, and access to store goods. However, the system
functioned very much like payday loans, in that the laborers went
into debt to the store and then never really received wages because
of the debt load. No matter how productive the laborers were, the
wages were never enough to get them out of debt, so there was no
just wage. Also, the laborers were exploited because of the debt

system. They always owed more than they could make up in labor or productivity, so they were still really slaves to the system. In a book by the same name, Denver said this about his experience, "I still couldn't understand how we could work so hard ever year, and ever year end up in the hole."[29]

Denver saw the depravity of the system and experienced the injustices of racism. He also experienced the deprivation of the system. Denver could not gain in this unjust system. Here is what he said:

> That ain't no bad life if your labor is for your own land. But it wadn't. And I don't guess that kinda life would be bad if it was somebody else's land, and you was getting paid. But I wadn't. Most folks these days ain't got no idea what it's like to be that poor.[30]

This system also withheld opportunities for growth and isolated Denver, so deprivation and a lack of development educationally, skill-wise, and personally were a consequence. Denver describes how his isolation kept him from knowing about schools for blacks, about opportunities to develop marketable skills, about the connection with the wider world and its resources that could have been available to him as he was growing up.

> You might be able to see how a colored man that couldn't read and didn't have a radio, no car, no telephone, and not even electricity might fall through a crack in time and get stuck, like a clock that done wound down and quit.[31]

---

29   Ron Hall, Denver Moore, and Lynn Vincent. *Same Kind of Different As Me*. (Nashville: Thomas Nelson, 2006), 29.

30   Ibid., 63.

31   Ibid., 64.

As Denver describes his journey into homelessness, he talks about how these factors contributed to his marginalization in a culture that values education, competency, success, and materialism. Who was responsible for this injustice? Denver was angry, but had mixed emotions in that he felt, on the plantation, he had work, a place to live, and food to eat, which was better than being homeless and jobless. These basic human needs are so important in addressing issues of justice and just compensation. As God sheds light on areas of darkness in our world, we see believers and non-believers respond to these areas of human need and issues of just wages.

Businesses struggle with how to be just and live for higher ideals than just making money. Some have great legacies and have missions that are in line with Kingdom imperatives. Henry Ford was idealistic and spiritual when he started the Ford Motor Company. He believed that profits should not be too high and that the car should be made available for everyone. So, he dropped his prices while others were raising them and while he was being sued by shareholders for reducing profits. He said,

> I don't believe we should make an awful profit on our cars. A reasonable profit is right, but not too much. I hold that it is better to sell a large number of cars at a reasonably small profit. ... I hold this because it enables a larger number of people to buy and enjoy the use of a car and because it gives a larger number of men employment at good wages. Those are the two aims I have in this life.[32]

From what I have read, Henry Ford was a man who had a Christian faith. He was a businessman in the business domain, but God used him to accomplish some of the ideals of the Kingdom. Henry was

---

32  James C. Collins and Jerry I. Porras, *Built to Last: Successful Habits of Visionary Companies*, 1st ed. (New York: HarperBusiness, 1994), 53.

committed to equity and a just distribution of wealth. He got some of his ideas from Ralph Waldo Emerson's essay "Compensation." Henry doubled the wages of the industry to five dollars a day for his employees and received a lot of criticism:

> *The Wall Street Journal* accused Henry Ford of "economic blunders if not crimes" which would soon "return to plague him and the industry he represents as well as organized society." In a naïve wish for social improvement, declared the newspaper, Ford had injected "spiritual principles into a field where they do not belong"—a heinous crime— and the captains of industry lined up to condemn "the most foolish thing ever attempted in the industrial world."[33]

Henry was accused of being too religious. He was mixing religion with business and the business sector did not approve. In the prophetic words of Jesus, he was being persecuted for righteousness.

Henry was a victim of the adage that says, no good deed goes unpunished. He, like William Wilberforce, felt he had two goals in life. Both centered around the theme of social justice, and contributing to the common good.

Today there are businesses like the Grameen Bank, founded by Muhammad Yunus, who earned a PHD from Vanderbilt in developmental economics. He started his bank to help the extreme poor become independent and self-sufficient financially. He won the Nobel Peace Prize for his efforts. Dr. Yunus, like Henry Ford, believes business is not just for profit-making but can be used to benefit others. He says, "To free market fundamentalists, social business might seem blasphemous. The idea of a business with

---

33    Ibid., 53.

objectives other than profits has no place in their theology of capitalism."[34] Yunus' motivation started with watching the poor be exploited by money lenders charging high interest rates and feeling ashamed of his country and wanting to help those who were suffering. He now believes that business can be aimed at social benefit, with social objectives, rather than just profit making.

## DEVELOPING ECONOMIC SYSTEMS

In Mark Kramer's book *Dispossessed*, he talks about the development of social systems in third world countries. These developing social systems are very vulnerable, like children in an early stage of development. The problem is that the other members of the system do not always function as nurturing parents that are benevolent in their dealings with these developing social systems. He says that many of the social systems are "informal settlements" which "Have . . . disease, land disputes, political injustice, corruption, gender inequalities, inadequate legal codes, . . . urban poverty which can seem hopeless and irrevocable."[35] As they struggle to become more structured or formal, they may or may not become organized in a way that is more ethical, just, and functional. The process of development can be healthy or unhealthy, as can be seen in family development. Some families neglect and abuse their children like these economic leaders can and often do. These processes—both family and social—need to be driven by people of good character who are invested in biblical ideals. They also need to understand developmental issues. For example, Kramer talks about the inequities between England and Kenya over the growth, processing, and sale of tea:

34   Mohammad Yunus, *Banker to the Poor: Micro-lending and the Battle Against World Poverty* (Public Affairs, 2003), 266.

35   Mark Kramer, *Dispossessed: Life in Our World's Urban Slums.* (Maryknoll, NY: Orbis Books, 2006), 4.

> While blame and root causes are debatable and complex, what's clear—and this is the main point here—is that Kenyans are not the real beneficiaries of their produce. Their finely cultivated beans and tea leaves stand among the best in the world. Just as under colonialism, outside interests are able to extract the wealth of Kenya's industry and, try as they might, Kenyans have too many disadvantages to compete globally.[36]

The Kenyans had come to a point of working hard and being productive, but the benefits were not going to them. The burden was not being balanced with the blessings, and so economic injustice was systemic for the Kenyans. How could they become less oppressed and find a more just wage?

That the relationships are benevolent and not exploitative is one of the main issues of the abuse of power and the lack of social justice or equity in these contexts. Colonialism was unjust because it was about taking through dominance and control. Those with power, competence, and resources need to be just and even invested in the well-being of those who are still developing. Development needs to be a part of their mission, just like with Henry Ford or Muhammad Yunus.

This is probably what Mott is talking about in terms of the world system/cosmos, a system that lacks the regeneration of the Holy Spirit and the purposes of a sovereign, good God. When the Kingdom of God reigns, those who are believers are obeying God and bringing the Kingdom to earth, through the power of God.

I do not think that people who do not believe have the power, direction, or the inspiration to bring about the kinds of social justice God requires. That does not mean that they cannot do good and significant works. God uses both believers and non-believers

---

36    Ibid., 74.

to accomplish His work. God does His will in spite of whether or not we are committed to obeying Him. The Church also sins and often needs reform to represent a just and loving God.

In the early part of this book, Robert Woodberry's research about missionaries who were committed to the well-being of those in developing nations was cited. These missionaries served during times of colonization, but their motives were to serve God. Woodberry found that they brought justice to developing nations.

Those who are developing also have to take responsibility for their part to be able to develop themselves. They have to find their own power in healthy ways.

Mahatma Gandhi is a great example of this. His leadership was essential in the development of India gaining independence from the British. Gandhi empowered the people through non-cooperation and nonviolent civil disobedience. He helped them find their voice or define themselves in ways that required the dominant culture to grant respect and independence. Yancey says in his mini-biography of Gandhi, "Gandhi stuck like a thorn in the side of the British because the standard means of control had no effect against his unorthodox protests."[37] Oppression and exploitation still requires some level of cooperation by the victim. Well-individuated people recognize this and are able to move away from control and oppression, but only through much difficulty.

Dr. Martin Luther King Jr. also had the strength to lead his people out from oppression by helping them find a voice through non-violent protesting, which invited suffering before change:

> When I went to Montgomery as a pastor, I had
> not the slightest idea that I would later become
> involved in a crisis in which non-violent resistance

---

37     Philip Yancey, *Soul Survivor: How My Faith Survived the Church*, 1st ed. (New York: Doubleday, 2001), 152.

would be applicable. I neither started the protest nor suggested it. I simply responded to the call of the people for a spokesman. When the protest began, my mind, consciously or unconsciously, was driven back to the Sermon on the Mount, with its sublime teachings on love, and to the Gandhian method of nonviolent resistance.[38]

Jesus calls us to bring reformation.

Strong leaders can lead others into healthy independence; they are able to lead partly because they are able to suffer well. Both Gandhi and King are great examples of men who could suffer well, without being controlled by fight-or-flight reactions to intense resistance, pain, and oppression. They accepted suffering as a part of the process of becoming differentiated, and their strong alliance with the oppressed gave strength emotionally, morally, and spiritually to others. Like Jesus, many of these leaders bring grace that creates justice, because of their willingness to suffer for others' well-being. Like Gandhi, King was not emotionally dependent on the goodwill of the dominant culture. He was able to accept criticism, rejection, and even punishment for his actions. He said, "One who breaks an unjust law must do so openly, lovingly and with a willingness to accept the penalty."[39]

The poor often feel powerless and then have a difficult time finding courage and healthy power. They need resources to become healthy—whether emotionally, relationally, intellectually, spiritually, or financially. In development work, the poor, marginalized, powerless, or developing have to find their own voice and competence to become healthy or individuated, especially in unhealthy systems. In healthy communities, as well as healthy families, everyone works towards sharing resources for the common good.

38  Ibid., 14.
39  Ibid.

## GRACE COMMUNITY & SOCIAL JUSTICE

Keller suggests that one of the only places that social justice fulfills the biblical imperatives is in the narrative of the second to fourth chapters of the book of Acts. In these chapters, you see that because believers were filled with the Holy Spirit and followed His leading, "there were no needy persons among them."[40] Keller believes that this was a fulfillment of Deuteronomy 15:4, "There should be no poor among you." Keller says, "This was the pinnacle of the 'social righteousness' legislation of the Old Testament, which expressed God's love for the vulnerable and His zeal to see poverty and want eliminated."[41]

The goal was a community of grace that came from faith, which brought provisions and healing. Empowerment was the biblical imperative given to people of faith in the fifteenth chapter of Deuteronomy, and it was fulfilled in this narrative in Acts because there were no needy among them. The fulfillment was in the sharing of resources for the empowerment of those in need, who were developing their newfound faith. Keller would say that the advantaged *disadvantaged themselves* for the disadvantaged, which created grace and justice.

With the issue of economic development, this is a never-ending process because of the young, broken, and poor. "There will always be some among you who are poor. That is why I am commanding you to share your resources freely with the poor and with other Israelites in need" (Deuteronomy 15:11). The book of Acts story is in the context of revival—with strong faith leaders, great Christian community, and an outpouring of the Holy Spirit. It also was short-lived, as the new believers were soon dispersed. But that may have been because the new believers were now established in their faith and could therefore move on in their lives

---

40    Keller, 59.

41    Ibid.

and penetrate the world with this newfound faith. They were launched into their callings.

In healthy families, there exists a grace community in that parents use their resources to empower their children. As a child grows and develops, they become spiritual, knowledgeable, educated, competent, and eventually valuable to others because they can contribute something of value to society. This is facilitated by a stable family that not only invests in their child's development, but expects them to attend to the tasks that will make them a healthy, independent, and valuable adult. Nagy calls this "positive entitlement" because children that receive this grace have a sense of positive indebtedness that motivates them to give freely to their own children. This creates a positive cycle where adults experience value and pass that value or dignity on to their children. This circularity is positive and reinforcing. When a person gives, they are loved and valued, which creates goodwill and cooperation, which invites more positive contributions. When children grow up valued and responsible, they become competent as adults in their basic life tasks, work, relationships, finances, family and spirituality. They *want* to give back. In our faith community, we have the same relational dynamic of positive entitlement in that "we love because he first loved us" (1 John 4:18).

# 9

## GRACE:
## THE PARADOX OF
## REDEMPTION IN THE AREA
## OF JUSTICE

I F GOD IS SO COMMITTED to justice, why is there all this injustice in life? How does it fit into His plan of redemption? I believe that, before we can effectively work towards righteousness and justice, we need to understand God's view of redemption and how it applies to our life.

When an injustice is committed, a debt is owed. Part of the definition of justice is about punishment for wrong-doing. It's about the right assigning of reward or punishment—about what is deserved. When a person does something wrong or fails to do the right thing, they owe a debt. In biblical terms that debt is sin, which requires a just wage. "For the wages of sin is death" (Romans 6:23. That debt has to be paid for justice to be fulfilled, or justice has not taken place. A just and righteous judge requires that debt to be paid in full. Accountability is central to the concepts of justice; people are responsible for their choices and lives and will be judged for what they do and do not do. And as we've seen, sin is not just about doing wrong, but about not doing what is right. This is where Dr. Blalock's insensitivity to Vivien's race and position caused injustice. He contributed to an evil and unjust system by being too passive. Biblically, it is about having a right relationship with God where we are accountable to Him—one where we trust and obey Him, so we are aware of what is required of us to live rightly. "Yes each of us will have to give a personal account to God" (Romans 14:12). Redemption is about the fact that somebody has to pay this debt and be accountable for when we fall short.

The central message of the Bible is that this debt is owed and that Christ came to be our Redeemer and pay that debt by dying for us because we could not pay it ourselves. John the Baptist says when seeing Christ, "there is the Lamb of God who takes away the sin of the world" (John 1:29). Redemption puts justice in the context of grace. So even though we deserve punishment we will be offered grace—undeserved forgiveness—through a debt that was paid for us by our Redeemer Jesus Christ who died in our place. What makes redemption meaningful is our understanding of the gravity of our debt, the consequences of that debt, and the relief being offered. That is what causes us to sing the song, "Amazing Grace." It is truly amazing that Christ was willing to pay this huge debt so we would not have to pay it.

In the criminal justice system, retributive justice is about the perpetrator of a crime paying for their own offense. They pay for it by spending time in prison, often so they will not victimize others anymore. However, without a sense of personal responsibility, remorse, ownership, and repentance—turning from wrong to doing what is right—we, as sinners, will continue to be perpetrators. God wants us to understand that justice protects us from evil even in ourselves.

As we receive redemption from our own sins, He then helps us to move to the right path. God wants to redeem us and to fellowship with us as the redeemed. In Isaiah God says, "I live in that high and holy place with those whose spirits are contrite and humble. I refresh the humble and give new courage to those with repentant hearts" (Isaiah 57:15). What is more humbling than facing our debt and finding that someone who loves us is willing to pay it for us when we deserve to suffer and be punished for it? I have watched so many people be overwhelmed with feelings of thankfulness when we paid off a payday or title loan in which they were suffering with a sense of powerlessness, guilt and shame. Christ paid off the greatest debt—our sin! Then He empowers us to become free and godly through knowing Him and seeking His will and Kingdom, free from our entanglements and free to do right.

## COUNTING THE COST OF COMMITMENT

Grace is a free gift but calls us into a relational commitment. Are you saved but not a disciple? Do you want your debt paid off so you can go to heaven, but have little interest in knowing God and doing His will on earth? One of the issues in maturity is commitment. A boy cannot be a man without adult commitments. To stop viewing women as "boy toys" and commit to marrying a woman will define a man and his roles, responsibilities, and tasks in life. When a person comes to Christ, they may desire forgiveness but not responsibility. Truth requires us to conform to God's will through submission, and Christ is both grace and truth.

I have had several people who got so far in debt that they thought the only way out was bankruptcy. I believe that in our culture, bankruptcy grants grace because it allows a person's debt to be forgiven. Some of these people have filed bankruptcy multiple times. You could say they received forgiveness but embraced it as "cheap grace" because they ignored their responsibility to change their financial habits. They did not repent or change their ways.

A commitment to do what is right is what becoming a disciple is all about. "Why do you call me Lord, and do not do what I say?" Jesus asks His followers (Luke 6:46). It seems that Jesus puts more emphasis on discipleship than evangelism, but both are needed. Both are a call to commitment—a call to know Jesus as Savior and a call to allow Him to rule. There is a cost to commitment, which each of us has to face. Are you willing to pay the price?

When I remarried at forty years old, I was told by my soon-to-be wife, "If you marry me, you have to be willing and committed to having more children." That was a big commitment, one I struggled with. Jesus warns us in Luke 14 that being a disciple is costly: "... You cannot be my disciple if you do not carry your own cross and follow me" (Luke 14:27). In cheap grace, the cross only represents what Christ did for us. In discipleship, grace also means how we obey and follow Him. Do you only want cheap grace—to be debt-free—but struggle to be a disciple? Commitment is costly!

## BROKENNESS LEADS US TO THE REDEEMER

The stories of Scripture communicate the significance of this great theme of redemption in the lives of people of faith. God desires us to see and understand our sinfulness and will expose it in our journey through our life, especially when we are close to a holy God who has drawn us to Himself. That is why there are so many narratives of brokenness in the Bible.

In David's well-known sin with Bathsheba, as he faces himself and God he says, "The sacrifice you want is a broken spirit. A broken and repentant heart O God, you will not despise" (Psalm 51:17). The realization of our own sinfulness breaks us of pride, which is our independence from God, His will, and His ways. Peter's trust in his own faithfulness leads him to boast of never deserting Christ, a test he later fails. Moses tries in his own strength to deliver Israel from the hand of oppression and becomes a murderer who is shunned by his own people who he desires to rescue. Paul, in his religious passion and self-righteousness, kills Christians and is confronted with his ignorance, sin, and betrayal of his God. He writes in 1 Timothy 1:15, "Jesus Christ came into the world to save sinners—and I was the worst of them all." Peter, Moses, and Paul all knew their own sinfulness, their need for forgiveness, and their dependency on God to live a righteous life. All of them experienced negative consequences for their sin. Most had years of waiting on God before being restored to positions of influence and service. They needed to be distant because of the hurt and alienation caused by their sin. These were broken men who knew their powerlessness over sin, but who understood the power of God's redemptive love. They saw their broken lives redeemed as they turned to their Redeemer for forgiveness and empowerment to live righteously.

Today, we have a generation of people who do not know they are sinners in need of redemption. They live in a culture that has not suffered like those in the past, that has never been broken by an economic depression and a world war. They boldly proclaim their goodness based on good works, philanthropy, inclusion, and saving the planet. These are good things, but salvation has never been about whether we are good or bad, it always has been about a need for a Redeemer who pays our debt. "For all have sinned and fall short of the glory of God" (Romans 3:23). There is no generation or person who does not need redemption. We cannot escape judgment of our sins by comparing ourselves with others. Paul was a self-righteous Pharisee who believed he was good and doing the right thing when he was killing Christians—until God confronted him on the road to Damascus and said, "Saul, Saul! Why are you persecuting me?" (Acts 9:4). That is when he came to know that he was a sinner, not a good person, but one who needed to be saved by God's grace.

We are often blind to our own sins and can see the sins of others more clearly than our own. As baby boomers, my generation could clearly see the sins of the generation who came before us, but we missed so many of our own sins. The younger generation views Christians as judgmental—people who are hateful and homophobic rather than loving. They see us as racist and sexist in comparison to their culture. This is sometimes true! We use others' sin and moral standards as an excuse not to love those who may be difficult or threatening. We Christians can be self-righteous and exclusive, not embracing those who are outside our tribe. Millennials, the younger generation, often believe they are better people who are not sinners in need of a Redeemer. But being a Christian is not about us but about Christ our Savior. He loved much better than any of us ever will. He also empowers Christians, through faith, to manifest His love and life in their lives.

Additionally, many of the younger generation do not believe in the judgment of God, but it is eminent. In fact, in this moment, there is a pandemic and economic downturn that is inviting personal reflection through the biggest shutdown I have ever seen or experienced. It does take faith in God's Word to believe that judgment will fall on sinners and to believe we are sinners. Because sin has consequences and evil destroys, judgment will come. That is the biblical view of judgment. Judgment is not just about threat and destruction—it comes from a loving God who protects His children from evil. So, fearing God, not just loving God, is a legitimate view of our faith. "Therefore knowing the fear of the Lord, we persuade men..." (2 Corinthians 5:11). We need to embrace Christ as Savior and Lord in order to love Him and obey His commands. To fear His judgment and repent will save us from His judgment. It is also God who saves us. That is why prayer and a message of warning is central for the salvation of this generation. Understanding redemption is so important, and knowing our Redeemer is the most important thing in life.

For many, redemption will come through brokenness, the consequences of sin—whether an economic crash, a plague, a major war, or the personal consequences from our own sin.

## RETRIBUTIVE JUSTICE OR BIBLICAL CORRECTION?

Everyone faces their sins in their life, but not all are broken in a way that leads to repentance and new life. In working with addicts, I have seen over and over again the clarity and insight that comes when people have a hard consequence from their bad behavior.

"I was such a jerk, no wonder she left me," says a husband who has been abusing alcohol and his wife for years. Before she left, he blamed her and his circumstances. It was everyone else's fault. Now he sees his part.

Usually consequences produce some grief or sorrow, but that does not always lead to repentance; it is just a consequence of the wrong that was done. Even though the alcoholic confesses or acknowledges his shortcoming, this is just the light that comes from the sobriety of grief. With so many people, consequences will enlighten them but not necessarily change their lives. Consequences always come from bad behaviors. Paul says, when developing and balancing his view of God's grace,

> Don't be misled. Remember that you can't ignore God and get away with it. You will always reap what you sow! Those who live only to satisfy their own sinful desires will harvest the consequences of decay and death (Galatians 6:7–8).

He also says that the consequences will not guarantee change:

> For the sorrow that is according to the will of God [consequences and grief] produces a repentance without regret, leading to salvation; but the sorrow [consequences and grief] of the world produces death (2 Corinthians 7:10).

So, the question is, when we have consequences, will our sorrow lead us to God and repentance or just emptiness and pain? Will we recognize God's discipline in our pain and turn to Him? Will we now seek God, who will give us life and life eternal, or will we stay independent from God and continue to look for love and life in all the wrong places.

PART II

# RESTORATIVE JUSTICE

# 10

## RETRIBUTIVE JUSTICE: LAW, CRIMINALITY, AND PUNISHMENT

THE CONSEQUENCES OF SIN are the punishment of sin. They are punitive because God has set up the universe in a way that sin leads to negative consequences, like death. Someone else may sin and cause your death, it may not be your fault at all, but there are consequences when we fall short. There are important exceptions and variations to this rule of sin which brings death, found in grace and God's redemption. The legal system works the same way in that, when a person commits a crime, there is a consequence. Legally, a crime has been committed that must be paid for. People who perpetuate crime also do not necessarily take personal responsibility for their wrong-doing, so then others have to hold them accountable and implement consequences. Criminals cause other people pain. Their victims are often hurt, angry, and want the perpetrators to be rewarded with pain, suffering, justice, or even vengeance. Justice is often viewed as a type of punishment—retributive justice. Howard Zehr says about retributive justice,

> Crime creates a moral debt which must be repaid and justice is a process of righting the balance. It is as if there is a metaphysical balance in the universe that has been upset and that must be corrected.[42]

Justice works on a spiritual level, but also on a human level. Only, with human relationships, emotions come into play so much more than just the legal aspect of what is owed.

Crime does victimize people and causes a certain violation of innocence. Most everyone who has been robbed, assaulted, or wounded feels violated. There is a balance that has been disrupted, a sense of loss of control, safety gone, and a wrong that needs to be put right. It is also very important for public safety that crime is dealt with, or society will lack peace and stability. "A sense of safety is a necessary ingredient in wholesome neighborhoods and thriving cities."[43] Order needs to be reestablished and justice is a part of reestablishing that order. But how is this facilitated through the criminal justice system? How is this justice approached? For sure, crime is a problem that needs to be addressed, but how do social justice, redemption, and other aspects of justice come into play?

## THE COMPLEXITY OF CRIME

In America, the criminal justice system is mainly about guilt and punishment. It is about the offender violating the laws for which they will need to be punished and suffer for their crime. Because of our worldview, we assume the individual to be autonomous and therefore completely responsible for their choice—a strong personal responsibility paradigm. They are then to be held responsible and punished without reference to other contributing factors

---

42  Howard Zehr, *Changing Lens: A New Focus for Crime and Justice* (Scottsdale: Herald Press, 2005), 74.

43  Heidi Unruh and Andy Rittenhouse, *Salt & Light: A Guide to Loving Knoxville* (Knoxville: Compassion Coalition Inc, 2009), 126.

to their behavior and attitudes. This goes back to earlier arguments in this book about overly-simplistic views of life that tend to be linear, rather than systemic. Many factors contribute to the health or pathology of any given situation. Even in Scripture, which has a strong emphasis on personal accountability, systemic views are represented.

There are many other factors that are seen as contributing to the sins of people. In the book of Proverbs, the economic environment is considered an influencing factor in a person's moral and relational behavior. "For if I grow rich, I may deny you and say, 'Who is the LORD?' And if I am too poor, I may steal and thus insult God's holy name" (Proverbs 30:9).

A person's family environment may contribute to their character, spirituality, and moral state, as psychologists see so plainly. Israel needed to confess not only their individual sins but the sins of their families to be healed. "But at last my people will confess their sins and the sins of their ancestors for betraying me" (Leviticus 26:40). This gives a social context as a factor for behavior as most psychologists and sociologists have found in their bodies of knowledge. Family grants a context for addressing definitions of dysfunction or pathology as variations in defining what is wrong.

We also know that the culture that people live in influences their behavior. Scripture supports this in so many places.

> Let's feast and get drunk, for tomorrow we die. Don't be fooled by those who say such things, for bad company corrupts good character. Come to your senses and stop sinning. For to your shame I say that some of you don't even know God, (1 Corinthians 15:32–33).

Paul is exhorting the Corinthians to separate from those who would be bad influences on them. This is also common knowledge with anthropologists or sociologists who study the effects of culture on human beings.

We know that there are many factors influencing behavior as knowledge has increased. Issues of addiction, mental illness, neighborhoods, economics, education, family stability, biochemistry, and genetics all contribute to our behavior and character; but our present system struggles with looking at justice in a systemic or holistic perspective. Zehr says,

> Justice is imaged as a blindfolded goddess holding a balance. The focus is on equity of process, not of circumstances. The criminal justice process claims to ignore social, economic, and political differences, attempting to treat all offenders as if they were equal before the law. Since the process aims to treat unequals equally, existing social and political inequities are ignored and maintained. Paradoxically, justice may thus maintain inequities in the name of equity.[44]

So, context is often ignored when looking at retributive justice, and then so are the issues of social justice which then perpetuate injustice. That is why the goddess of justice on our book cover is peeking out from her blindfold. She is looking at more than impartial judgment when implementing the sword of justice.

We struggle with keeping knowledge in separate categories, partly because it makes life simpler and less complex to deal with. Compartmentalizing knowledge is often a part of our adult training, but it also keeps us making bad decisions that overlook major factors like context. Zehr says,

---

44    Zehr, 79.

Because guilt is narrowly defined, centering on individual behavior, it allows us to ignore the social and economic roots, and contexts of crime. We thus attempt to create justice by leaving out many of the relevant variables.[45]

Scripture addresses this complexity through the Genesis narrative of Adam and Eve falling out of fellowship with God and creating original sin, which then permeates all of creation with evil and corruption. This scriptural view of evil is simple and yet so complex because it covers all systems, not just the individual and his or her choices.

To address many systemic problems, we have to deal with many factors not just the legal or moral issues. In the story of Bob and Julie, they are both sinning and need to be accountable for their behavior. However, there is a context to their behavior which is complicated. Their behavior really only makes sense in the context of their histories, relational dynamics, emotions, circumstances, biochemistry and spirituality; and that is also where the solutions will be found to their marital problems.

Os Guinness accuses evangelicals of being lazy thinkers in his book *Fit Bodies, Fat Minds*. He says that we have given up the part of the great commandment of worshiping God with all our mind. We want a simplistic faith that denies the complexities of our life—which require more knowledge, competency and personal growth on our part as believers. He quotes John Schurr:

> The brute fact remains that this country, which has produced more Protestant believers than any other, has also produced fewer powerful Protestant theologians and theological-social theorists than any other major Protestant country. The evangelical leaders

---

45  Ibid., 72–73.

are not equipped intellectually to think through complex social issues of the times and offer genuinely new and promising solutions.[46]

Guinness's point is that we are not being obedient to God because of our lazy thinking. Justice is a complicated subject because of all the variables, and the implementation of dealing with crime is not simple. Court systems are beginning to broaden; we now have family courts, mental health courts, and recovery options for addictions. These more specialized justice options will help deal with the complexity of crime and its effects on the victim, offender, and society.

\*\*\*\*

This week I saw an ex-offender—a man who spent five years in prison for assault and robbery. He was struggling with finding a job to support himself, his girlfriend, and his daughter. He was abandoned by his parents and went to live on the street at ten years old. He joined a gang who became his family. He did not expect to live to be twenty years old. He was now forty years old, angry, and hopeless. He was focused on the pain in his life.

When I asked him about God he said, "I am unhappy every day, angry over not having a job, not being able to pay the bills, feeling my life is bad, and it is hard to believe that there is a God who loves me and cares about me."

He struggled to have hope. He struggled to have faith that life could be better. He was not educated or trained to have marketable skills. He was trying to love his girlfriend, who had a job but still did not make enough money to pay the bills and was fighting a disease. Life was not as simple as just making the right choices because he was now wanting to not live a life of crime.

---

46  Os Guinness, *Fit Bodies, Fat Minds: Why Evangelicals Don't Think and What to Do About It* (Grand Rapids, MI: Hourglass Books, 1994), 13.

He needed financial assistance, a job, someone to care about him and his family. He had tattoos all over him including his face, and needed them removed to get a job in the public arena. I gave him a Bible and some money, but that is hardly enough to bring restoration, amends for years of neglect, and motivation to overcome the obstacles and live a godly life. The consequences of his and his family's behaviors were leaving him hopeless, as if he lived under a curse which started generations ago but was infecting him today. He had been negatively entitled through neglect and abuse and now wanted to become positively entitled through Christ and the grace offered to him. Life and justice are very complex. He needed resources, hope, faith, love, and so much more. He also needed preventive work that comes from having a healthy family. Can we provide resources for under-resourced youth? What does justice really look like?

There are many questions to answer in this area of retributive justice. Who is the victim? What crimes are so severe that restoration is limited or not possible? Who is responsible for what in the justice process? Is dealing with sin as important as dealing with crime? What are the goals of the criminal justice system? What part is the state to play, and what part are the family, Church, and community to be involved in?

## CRIME AS RELATED TO WHO?

Zehr says that the original purpose of "incarceration was to meet society's need for punishment and protection while encouraging reformation of offenders."[47] In this process key players began to be marginalized and key processes ignored. Because of that, the system began to fail in its missions. The focus became the offender against the state.

---

47    Zehr, 63.

According to Zehr, the following assumptions have defined the process of justice:

1. crime is essentially *lawbreaking;*
2. when a law is broken, justice involves establishing *guilt;*
3. so that just deserts can be meted out;
4. by inflicting *pain;*
5. through a *conflict* in which *rules* and intentions are placed above outcomes.[48]

The problems with this model are that it leaves out so many of the essentials of dealing with human relationships, it leaves out God, and it depersonalizes the process of crime and the people involved.

The offense of a crime is against a victim, but that is quickly shifted to be seen as an offense against the state. So, key elements for restoration like confession, repentance, and making the wrongs right are also removed from the offender's responsibility and given to the state. This further breaks down community and a social fabric that is already negatively affected by crime in our cities. Viewing the debt of crime as being owed to the state and not the victim, the community, or even God, distances and disconnects those living in our community by inviting them to be less personally accountable for their actions. This disconnection also breaks down communication, which then gives rise to speculation rather than a good information exchange. Alienation and isolation are some of the natural consequences of crime, but they are exacerbated by this process which marginalizes the offender—who often is struggling with becoming a healthy part of the community—even more, and allows the victim to vilify and depersonalize the criminal through imagination rather than the context of the offender's story.

48   Ibid., 63.

There is another approach that contrasts with *retributive* justice. It is called *restorative* justice, and it aligns much more closely with some of the redemptive and restorative processes that have already been mentioned in this book.

In our community, a person named Jim Fish began to facilitate restorative processes in the public school system. He worked to resolve conflicts through "conferencing"—having kids speak face to face to work out their own conflicts rather than punishing them. They learned a process to take responsibility for their wrongs, own their offenses, make their wrongs right, and restore relationships. Jim is a Christian and so part of this process was forgiveness—debt was to be forgiven rather than used to marginalize the offender. Each person has a part to play if restorative justice is to work.

When the focus is on the offender, others in the system often do not feel or believe they need to behave themselves. During the time I worked on restorative justice in our juvenile justice system, I became well aware that the whole system needed to be accountable, not just the perpetrator.

\*\*\*\*

About a month after I started working in restorative justice, one of my sons got arrested as a juvenile. God has a sense of humor! My son was car-hopping at a local mall. He and his friends were running over cars as they approached speed bumps. These boys were victimizing others and breaking the law. They ran over an off-duty policeman's car as he was teaching his son to drive. He was angry and probably embarrassed in front of his son. They obviously didn't care how they affected others; they were just out to have fun.

At 11:30pm an officer called me saying he had my son in the back of his car.

I drove to the mall and found he had come back to the scene of the crime to be loyal to his friends. He had run and escaped but returned when one of his friends did not escape. The police officer was holding him and wanted him to tell who else had been with him. My son, who is very loyal, did not want to name anyone.

I told him he had to answer honestly, because he was in the wrong and needed to respect authority, but I could see it hurt him very much to feel disloyal by telling on his friends.

Then, while I was talking to the one officer, the off-duty policeman started swearing at my son.

My wife, who never backed away from protecting her family, said to him, "Like you never did anything wrong when you were a kid."

A female officer grabbed her.

I approached and she let go.

The police then wrote up my wife but ignored their off-duty police officer's inappropriate behavior.

Since I just happened to know the police officer who was over these officers, I called him the next morning. He said the off-duty officer was out of line and asked if I wanted any disciplinary action taken against him. I said no and was more interested in observing how the system worked from inside it.

In the next meeting, we were asked to sign a confession without legal representation. We were told if we did there would only be a minor fine of $500 for both boys and they would receive help for their misconduct. In court, the fine was raised to $3,200 and the other boy was going to jail if he did not pay it. I lent him the money.

To make a long story short, every stage of the process was corrupt with officials lying and manipulating to get the perpetrators—my son and his friends—convicted in their violation of the law. Their rights were ignored! For those in the system, their job was to get the boys to own their wrong-doing, but they ignored their own wrongs.

It is easy for us, in our humanity, to make our jobs and responsibilities more important than a relationship with God or others. Of course, I didn't even know if any of the people I encountered in the legal system were believers, or whether Jesus was Lord of their lives, but it did not appear He was. Sins of ignorance go with not knowing God, and when people don't know who they are and where their true significance comes from, position and responsibility become more important than pleasing their God.

All people are created in His image, but believers are "new creatures" in Him. We begin to live from a position of significance rather than one where we have to strive to earn our worth. We are significant before God, but still experience being valued when we do a good job. We live on this earth with the social systems we are engaged in, and so affirmations, validations, and significance are important from these sources. As Christians, we are not Gnostics separating the spiritual from the material, but we prioritize our relationship with our God. Our Lord is not separate from our lives; He works within the callings we live in. God is our main source of significance and life, but that comes from a devotion to Him that also informs us of who we truly are. Then, through faith in Him, we do what is right and learn how to do it. As we learn to worship the One who is worthy of our worship, we also gain a sense of our own true worth!

I ended up writing a report about the judge's and officers' unethical behavior in the context of restorative justice. It amazed me that they expected the young boys to be moral, but were either ignorant or just immoral themselves and never acknowledged their own wrongs. The people in the justice system were ignoring relationships, ethics, and morals. They were not violating the law themselves, but their own rules and God's laws were being violated.

My conclusion was that, in doing restorative justice, dealing with sin is just as important as dealing with crime. It is important that we have authority figures (structural authority) that hold those breaking the law accountable, and their jobs are very important in establishing order in our society. We all need to do God's will (Romans 13:1–3) and respect authority as established by God. But authority figures are also to do God's will, God's way (spiritual authority).

Jesus had authority. It was not structural but spiritual and relational. He challenged structural authority by challenging the religious system of the day. When authority figures ignore spiritual and relational authority, is that abuse of their authority? Jesus thought it was.

Sins of ignorance affect all of us, even in how we can use morals and laws to judge others and justify our own sin! Authority figures have a responsibility to be people of good character and lead by example. They also need to be held accountable for lying and manipulation if they are to be creditable.

# 11

## RESTORATIVE JUSTICE: ACCOUNTABILITY, REPARATION, AND REDEMPTION

T HERE ARE TOO MANY AREAS of contrast and complexity between restorative justice and retributive justice to cover in this book, but I will talk about a few of them to move us in the direction of restorative justice. This is a quote that was written to introduce restorative justice in the manual we produced for the Department of Labor: "Restorative justice is about making the wrong right in the context of relationships, rather than just the criminal justice system."[49] One of the main contrasts between retributive justice and restorative justice is that retributive justice is punitive, where restorative justice is a commitment to restorative processes. Restorative justice is about the relational dynamics that create, maintain, and restore healthy interpersonal relationships. Societies that are healthy have respect and trust maintained

---

49   One Stop Center, Pima County Community Services, and Employment and Training Department, Youth Employment and Re-entry Network (YEARN), "Restorative Justice Handbook", (Tucson: by the author), 6.

in their community. Restorative justice works to restore these values and relational dynamics to the community when they are lost or broken.

## POINTS OF RESTORATIVE JUSTICE

Here are some of the main points that we used to define the contrasts of these two processes, taken from the "Restorative Justice Handbook":

A. The victim is the person who is hurt most by the crime, but many are affected including family members, the offender, neighbors and the community.

B. For restorative justice to be effective crime needs to be addressed as first violating people and relationships. The state is secondary and impersonalizes the process of justice as well as moves it towards retributive justice.

C. Restorative justice is basically about relationships: how to restore them, how to bring ownership for offenses, how to do restitution, how to bring healing, how to create responsibility and prevention, and how to reconcile. Where retributive justice is about punishment, paying for the offense. It is about giving pain for an offense. It is often about vengeance. However, retributive justice is also about removing unsafe people who commit crimes from the community to attempt to make the community safe. In contrast restorative justice focuses more on whether a person is now capable of being a safe person in the community and removal is based on issues of maturity, sobriety, ownership, level of the intensity of the crime and true repentance that allows people to be safe around them.

D. Restorative justice has to do with the context of people's lives not just responsibility and accountability. It looks at all the factors contributing to crime: family, addiction, neighborhood, education, jobs, as well as personal responsibility. Can a healthy support system be established?

E. Restorative justice empowers victims to define their needs and allows offenders to understand the harm they have done, as well as taking appropriate responsibility for their crime. It invites confession and forgiveness in relationships.

F. Restorative justice is not vindictive but may be painful and costly. Shame and amends are often part of making things right that were made wrong through the crime. Both the victim and the offender play a part in restoration and both parts are very important.

G. The community is responsible for its own welfare and required to hold offenders accountable and love them back to restoration. We as the community are responsible to bring healing and safety to our city.

H. Those who are marginalized and alienated because of their wrongs may only get worse if they do not personally make necessary changes and continue through the prison system. They become a drain on the society and non-contributing members.

I. The goals of restorative justice are
  1. to make wrongs right
  2. to empower the victim by meeting their needs through bringing information, validation, restitution, safety and justice

3. to have the offender repair harm
4. to address the needs of the offender: mental health, competencies, education, job readiness, social skills, spiritual development, and the need to belong and contribute to a healthy social network.

J. The outcome of restorative justice can be public safety, accountability, that all are connected to a loving community, inclusion and effective recovery and restoration. To reduce recidivism is also a major goal as a by-product of the successful implementation of these processes.[50]

The ideal is that the offender sees the harm they have caused, owns it, is willing to make it right and conference with the victim to find ways of paying this debt off. Zehr says about the offender:

> You have done wrong by violating someone. You have an obligation to make that wrong right. You may choose to do so willingly, and we will allow you to be involved in figuring out how that should be done. If you do not choose to accept this responsibility, however, we will have to decide for you what needs to be done and will require you to do it.[51]

The difficulty with restorative justice is that the victim often does not want to have anything to do with the offender who has wounded them. In most cases, community service plays a much bigger role than the face-to-face dialogue of conferencing. The offender pays their amends to the community rather than directly to the victim. For juvenile offenders to make amends and understand their debt needs to be paid back, community service is the

---

50   YEARN, 7–8.
51   Zehr, 198.

main venue in most cases. We worked with Knoxville, Tennessee, because they appeared to have the best faith-based restorative justice ministry for juveniles in the country. In Tucson, we have several places where conferencing happens—in schools, juvenile justice (ADJC), etc. This is a scripted process where both the victim and offender are asked questions in the presence of each other. The conferencing process is very personal with the victim and offender being together in the same room. It also includes those who are most affected, like family, friends, and meaningful relationships.

Victims of crime do not necessarily see any relational responsibilities. In fact, because of the trauma and pain, they may be extremely averse to working a restorative process. These processes are found where community is valued. In Tucson, the main model for restorative processes has been facilitated by Andrew Revering, who brought us this model, developed by the Maori culture of New Zealand. He was originally introduced to it by Sergeant Terry O'Connell of the New South Wales Police Department of Australia. It often takes someone who is a strong leader and very invested in the process to bring people together to work the process of reconciliation or restoration. Of course, the more severe the crime, the greater the obstacles and the harder it is to come together. Safety and trust are major goals in this process.

\*\*\*\*

A few years ago, while I was running a Christian counseling agency, we saw a story in the paper and on the news of a man who, while intoxicated, hit another man on a motorcycle and almost killed him. What was so unusual about this story were the elements of restorative justice. George (not his real name) had been drinking at a bar and left the bar early in the morning very drunk. He hit Ron on his way to work and Ron was believed to be dead at the scene of the accident. An EMT found that Ron was not dead but had most of the bones in his lower body broken and his larynx crushed. If Ron had died, George would have had a mandatory long prison sentence.

As they went to court, Ron met George with no ill-will. He stood and told the judge that he did not want George to go to prison, but wanted George to help him with his rehabilitation, which was extensive. The judge wanted to sentence George to nine years in prison, but Ron asked for amends work instead. George went to a work-release program for one year while he watched and helped Ron with his recovery. How do you forgive a person who has caused irreparable damage to your body?

George had pain. He wept deeply through the interview we had and expressed a lot of shame in the context of receiving so much grace. George was blown away by the grace given him by Ron. I had the privilege to interview the whole family within the first year of this accident. George's family were evangelical Christians and had been praying for George's sobriety and that he would get right with God.

Both Ron and his wife had strong faith, and their faith seemed to help them through this huge trial. Ron had been arrested as a young man and spent fifteen years in and out of prison. He started his incarceration with a drunk-and-disorderly offense, and he felt that prison was not the place for George. He was very forgiving and gracious. He was much more interested in restorative justice rather than retributive justice, but there were strong feelings to overcome, especially from Ron's wife.

I believe this situation was orchestrated by God and that in His sovereignty, He brought about these processes. However, I believe it is also the responsibility of the faith community to work towards these divine purposes and values because they are so much a part of the Kingdom of God. God is aggressive in giving His imperatives about justice, and the Church is guilty of sins of omission when they ignore these strong commands of Scripture. We ended up naming our scholarship fund in the counseling agency to honor Ron.

Zehr, who comes from a Mennonite background, sees the Church or faith community having responsibility for the leadership of restorative justice in their communities. He says, "the Church has a special responsibility in this process."[52] He looks at this as the Church inviting alternative forms of justice, often outside the systems of our world. He uses the exhortations where Paul talks about Christians not taking Christians to court, but settling their disputes themselves. The sad part of this is that, in the fifty years I have been working in the Christian community, I see Christians being mainly avoidant and sometimes punitive, not restorative in their orientation towards resolving issues of conflict, sin and injustice.

It takes courage to do reconciliation work and you have to believe it is worth the work as part of your call. We as believers have to lead in our own lives and communities if we are to touch the lives of the rest of our community, which will take humility and surrendering to the will of God. Zehr says that we need, "to get our own act together."[53] How else will we be able to demonstrate the redemption of God over sin, the curse, and fallen humanity?

---

52  Ibid., 226.
53  Ibid.

# 12

## SHALOM:
## JUSTICE AND GRACE
## TOGETHER CREATE RIGHT
## RELATIONSHIP

RESTORATIVE JUSTICE HAS TO do with restoring a "right" order to relationships. What is a right order of things in this world? For many who write about justice, that right and just order has to do with God's Kingdom purposes being manifest, and has been consistently related to the concepts of *shalom* in the Old Testament. Zehr says,

> *Shalom* defines how God intends things to be. God intends people to live in a condition of "all rightness" in the material world; in interpersonal, social, and political relationships; and in personal character. There can be no *shalom* when things are not as they ought, and the absence of *shalom* is at the heart of the criticisms the Old Testament prophets leveled at God's people. The vision of *shalom* also shapes the hopes and promises for the future.[54]

---

54    Ibid., 132.

Most of the time *shalom* is translated as "peace" in the Old Testament, but it means so much more. It relates to the divine purposes of God and His reign with His people. As people of faith follow God and desire to hear His call and obey His voice, the old order of the cosmos is replaced by the "new," which is a part of Christ's redemption of the world. This is the concept of "Thy Kingdom come, Thy will be done on earth as it is in heaven" (Matthew 6:9). It means that God is bringing His Kingdom and we are growing into it as we learn who He is and who we are to be in all areas of our life. Here is what Tim Keller says about the word *shalom*: "*Shalom* means complete reconciliation, a state of the fullest flourishing in every dimension—physical, emotional, social, and spiritual—because all relationships are right, perfect, and filled with joy."[55]

I believe that God is working at several levels to bring about His *shalom*. He works through common grace to accomplish His purposes in our culture, for the benefit of all. He also works through special grace as He brings humanity to a saving faith in Jesus Christ, which also brings transformation and *shalom* as the promise of heaven and eternal life yet to come. Christ will return and establish His Kingdom!

From the beginning of Scripture, we get glimpses of God's intentions and have ideas of what life is to be all about. Plantinga says that since St. Augustine, we have had some understanding of *shalom* and the way things are supposed to be.

> For central in the classic Christian understanding of the world is a concept of the way things are supposed to be. They ought to be as designed and intended by God, both in creation and graceful restoration of creation. They are supposed to include peace that

---

55   Keller, 174.

adorns and completes justice, mutual respect, and deliberate and widespread attention to the public good.... The webbing together of God, humans and all creation in justice, fulfillment, and delight is what the Hebrew prophets call *shalom*.[56]

*Shalom* is to exist at every area of life—individual, marital, family, community, political, national, worldwide, and with all of creation. I think sometimes though, it has to work in each sphere and start with the smallest units. Families that cannot structure a healthy order into their own lives will infect others and those pathologies will infect still others. Things like poor mental health, addiction, divorce, abuse, neglect, affairs, debt, unruly adolescents, and the symptoms of dysfunction in families do infect other families as well. Sin and disease will not disappear, just because we work toward creating *shalom* and look to Christ for our redemption, but the gospel is about the fall, sin, and its consequences eventually being eliminated.

God is determined to restore His original intentions of a creation that is "good." Plantinga says, "God wants *shalom* and will pay any price to get it back."[57] This includes the death of His Son and He also calls us to pay prices in taking up our crosses to bring about *shalom*. It is a large part of our mission or call in life. To create *shalom* on all levels is part of the purpose of the Christian life. So, we work towards the definitions of *shalom*, to see families are sober, united in partnership, loving and affirming, validating and empowering, faithful and filled with dignity instead of shame. We start where we live, at the family level, and move in faith so that we become functional and healthy and begin to positively infect the community with *shalom*. Of course, all

---

56    Cornelius Plantinga, *Not the Way It's Supposed to Be: A Breviary of Sin* (Grand Rapids, MI; Leicester, Eng.: Eerdmans; Apollos, 1995), 8, 10.

57    Ibid., 199.

families struggle with health and disease, function and dysfunction, sin and godliness—but the healthier a family is, the more godly characteristics are manifest. In this life there is ambiguity—the upside comes with a downside; there is good and bad, strength and weakness, right and wrong—in all of us. Confession and humility bring forgiveness and honor. So, acceptance, forgiveness and love are as important as working towards truth, justice, and righteousness. Serenity and *shalom* need to be embraced in this world for His Kingdom to come and for His will to be done.

\*\*\*\*

Julie and Bob came into my office with a lot of dysfunction, reacting to each other in negative circularity, or loops. *Shalom* could not be seen in their marriage. However, as they began to work over time, each invested first in the fabric of their relationship with God and then with each other. Months later there was still some hurt and mistrust, but both sat quietly, peacefully holding hands.

I asked what had happened.

Bob said, "It's Julie's fault," with a smile on his face. "She is making me love her again. She is kind and responsive and easy to love."

Julie protested, "You're sober and humble and you are listening to me!"

The circularity of the relationship had changed from reactive to responsive, from threatening to secure, from punitive to rewarding. Both Julie and Bob, with God's help, had created this new relational fabric, which the theologians might call *shalom*. It sure was a lot more peaceful. They still had stress and character flaws and conflicts, but there were tastes of His Kingdom in this marriage. It was a lot of work for them to humble themselves and give up their pride, hurt, and anger, to own their part, and to take responsibility to be intentionally-loving, good, reciprocating, and spiritual. It was also going to take work to maintain this unity and partnership in their marriage. The healing or restoration of this marriage was complex and a few paragraphs cannot represent the process of reconciliation that took place, but like the broad-brush concepts of *shalom*, they can point in the right direction.

## SHALOM AND THE GRACE COMMUNITY

For justice to take root, it needs to be rooted in grace. For a family or a society to move from the way it *is* to the way it *should be* often takes faith and love. Mott says, "Justice carries out what love motivates. It is 'the order which love requires.' As order, it shapes the kind of society to which love points."[58] That happens when believers decide to follow Christ and love others well.

One of the great stories of a radical turnaround based on justice and grace is the story of Wayne Alderson, who worked in a Pittsburgh steel foundry. To get a taste of *shalom* we need godly systems and godly people of great character creating them. Wayne Alderson's story, *Stronger Than Steel*, written by R.C. Sproul, gives us a taste of Kingdom transformation.

Wayne had worked his way up the ladder in the Pittron Steel Foundry to the place of vice president in charge of operations. However, he stepped into a huge conflict. Management and labor were fighting. The company had lost six million dollars and was about to go bankrupt as a strike broke out. The atmosphere of the company was combative and the hostility levels were extremely high. Labor mistrusted management and management was very embittered towards labor. It was a loop with both sides entrenched in their unyielding positions.

---

58  Mott, 54.

During that time, Wayne went to a church retreat where he was challenged to put his "...faith and values to the test in the real world. They were told to come out from under the shelter of their steeples and into the market place."[59] The speaker likened Christians to Native Americans who lived on a reservation. If they were going to live out their faith, they needed to come off the reservation where they were safe and hidden away. The speaker exhorted them to live out their faith in the domain where it touched the people of the world. For Wayne, that was the marketplace—a place of business—and Wayne was challenged.

There could not have been a better time for him to hear this exhortation. He formed a plan to turn the foundry around and found that many thought he was foolish. He knew that his faith had to be a faith of substance and not empty words. So, Wayne began to do things like meet his employees at the front door, shake their hands and learn their names. Great change comes through sacrifice! His goal was reconciliation, to mend the mistrust and broken promises between labor and management. Their conflicts had caused them to become enemies, when they needed to be partners in their tasks. Alderson made the commitment to restore these broken relationships and decided he would do his part even if they did not respond in kind. "We must take the first step and—if necessary—the second and the third until things start to change. We're responsible for what we do, not for what they do in response."[60]

Wayne got involved with labor but, as you will hear, perhaps overlooked the owners and management in his mission to bring *shalom* to this volatile company.

Wayne began to grant a grace that was about human dignity. He recognized that many of the workers felt devalued by management's

---

59    R. C. Sproul, *Stronger Than Steel: The Wayne Alderson Story*, 1st ed. (San Francisco: Harper & Row, 1980), 49.

60    Ibid., 60.

confrontational style and he stepped up to correct that. He gave value to men who had not been valued in the past. He talked with them, worked alongside of them, visited them when they were sick, learned all of their names, and began to change the inequities that he could recognize. He valued people over machines and profits and began living those values out in relationship to the men he worked with.

Wayne gave a grace that gave honor or respect to people who had not experienced respect from management. He chose to grant that grace because of his faith and his belief in the value of people, who were made in God's image. The reason this was grace was that many in management would not have granted this type of value to the employees. They would have framed it in the perspective that *respect is earned, not given.* However, Wayne yielded to a biblical passage that says we are to give more honor to those who receive less honor (1 Corinthians 12:23). Perhaps he saw management as perpetrating injustice and was called to right that wrong. His job was also to have labor bring more value to the company through productivity.

Justice is about value judgments. Systems define what is valuable and how rewards like money, honor, and other recompenses are to be given. So often a person in a system will be overlooked and not honored because the system invalidates them; like the example given earlier about Vivien Thomas as the black medical assistant who was invalidated because of race and a lack of academic achievement; or the poor in Bangladesh that Dr. Yunus advocates for by operating a bank that grants dignity and financial empowerment. In the case of Wayne Alderson, he recognized that the workers who had the most difficult work were the "chippers," the workers who used thirty-pound hammers to chip away defects from large steel castings. This job was one of the hardest, dirtiest, and most demanding. It took the most strength, but was the least rewarded. Wayne recognized this and intentionally vali-dated the men who did this work.

This is what Scripture exhorts believers to do in order to create a grace community that is equitable. Paul says,

> In fact, some of the parts that seem weakest and least important are really the most necessary. And the parts [people with gifts] we regard as less honor-able are those we clothe with the greatest care.... So God put the body together in such a way that extra honor and care are given to those parts that have less dignity. This makes for harmony among the members, so that all the members care for each other equally (1 Corinthians 12:22–25).

Recompense in this steel mill took the form of honor given by the vice president through personal care. Wayne functioned like the "undercover boss" who gets involved with his employees, learns their stories, and cares about them. He went and worked with the chippers.

The difficulty with this is that many who need grace and dignity keep inviting punishment because their behaviors may be more of a liability than an asset. I have worked in the Jesus Movement where many who came to live in community were there to be taken care of, contributing very little. They needed grace, but also truth to grow. Some of them were constantly creat-ing conflict and messes that others who were higher-functioning had to clean up. A romantic view of their worth would soon turn into a tragedy through experiencing their brokenness as a liabil-ity. Many in the Jesus Movement went from deficits to assets as they grew in faith and became contributors rather than takers. So, from a value point of view, they at times were really worth-less in their contributions, and even created deficits that had to be overcome to love them well. But, as believers, they had potential and value in Christ.

In the book *Same Kind of Different As Me*, it is a woman named Deborah who loves and values Denver, the homeless black man who grew up a sharecropper. It is her grace that gives him a place and inclusion that brings healing to his soul. It is not that Denver earns this validation or dignity, but it is granted and then creates a community of grace in their family. As he responds and lets down his guard, his worth and dignity do show up and make a difference. Denver then pays it forward in helping the homeless through fundraising.

This is what also happens in the *Stronger Than Steel* story. Wayne invites a community of grace that, through his love and leadership, bonds the company. In a 21-month period, "Operation Turnaround" brought about these results:

1. Sales went up 400%.
2. Profits rose to 30%.
3. Employment went up 300% (the work force grew from 300 to over 1,000 employees).
4. Productivity rose 64%.
5. Labor grievances declined from as many as twelve per week to one per year.
6. Chronic absenteeism virtually disappeared.
7. The quality of the product became "the best in the history of the plant."[61]

*Shalom* from a grace community had taken place at a steel foundry. Wayne also started a Bible study that was extremely well-attended and made a difference in the personal lives of the men he worked with. Truth was being received in this grace community. They were now profitable as a company to the tune of six million dollars, but the real accomplishment was the atmosphere of the plant. It was one of goodwill and cooperation, where people were

---

61    Ibid., 72–73.

working together for common purposes that benefited all of them. They were valuable in every way. Respect was also earned and required as the community of grace grew and developed *shalom*. This was not just the soft values of grace, but they were foundational for everyone to contribute and become valuable in their common mission at work.

In R.C. Sproul's chapter called "The Penalty for Overachievement" the negative consequence for this now-productive company was that it was sold, and Wayne lost his job. In my opinion, Wayne overlooked management's need for grace and truth. After all, they were a part of this system that badly needed God's grace and truth, but I did not hear that Wayne focused on them as a part of his call. The profit motive in business often usurps God's call to stewardship and divine purposes. Sin permeates all of life and, even though Christ is now the ruler of the universe, most do not submit to His leadership without conversion and transformation. We all have a choice of who we serve: ourselves, the system we are in, or Christ. Wayne seemed to have missed the fact that the owners needed grace and Christ's rule in their lives, and he paid a price in experiencing betrayal and disrespect. Sproul comments on this by saying,

> The object of (work) labor is not greed. The earth is to be replenished and adorned by human labor. To exploit and pollute the earth is a monstrous sin against creation: to oppress human workers evokes the wrath of God. . . . To banish or exile God from the work world is to defy God's intrinsic right to rule His creation.[62]

The owners needed a relationship with Christ based on His grace so that dignity—not greed or disloyalty—would permeate the

---

62   Ibid., 184.

community. The Kingdom rule of Christ needs to be established in the hearts of all for *shalom* to transform a whole system. God is the one who saves us and we all miss opportunities.

****

It is common when you advocate for the powerless that you end up allying with the victim against the perpetrator. The injustice engages the advocate in angry feelings against the perpetrator—the one who abused their power. It is difficult not to take up the offense that the abuser of power gives when you are invested in the life of the victim.

Did Wayne have hurt and resentment against his employer? Did he trade evil for evil with them? He acknowledges that he almost always obeyed authority, but disobeyed by not coming to a mandatory meeting because they betrayed him. Was that a sin on his part? When Wayne came to face the new employer, they flew him to their headquarters and were willing to compromise with his leadership style. Yet, he resigned and was not actually fired. In fact, they told him he was one the best managers in the world. However, they *were* challenging his call and mission. And, in my opinion, it seems possible he couldn't live with that invalidation. What we do not get, in his story, is their story.

There is a little formula to keep in mind: *The mission cannot be taken captive by the rewards of doing mission, and the mission cannot seduce the called from the Commissioner.* Christ, as the Caller, is always more important than mission or the blessings received in having His favor.

In restorative justice, the conference between the victim and perpetrator has many purposes. One of them is to allow the victims to see the human side of the person who is now owning their offense and telling their story. Most of the time, when we are victimized, we vilify the perpetrator and they become a monster rather than a human being who is fallen and in need of redemption.

There's a show on TV called *The Redemption Project with Van Jones*. In one episode, a family severely victimized by a drunk driver who almost mortally wounded their daughter, meets with the offender. Their lives are now changed forever because of this victimization and their daughter will never be the same. They have tremendous losses caused by an addict who they do not know. They had not heard from the perpetrator for over ten years and were sure this monster did not care how she had affected them.

The story was that the drunk driver had gone to prison, gotten sober, stabilized, and wanted to contact the family, but was prevented contact by the legal system as well as her own shame. Shame causes people to distance and often hide from those they have hurt, and perpetrators often have self-hatred as they reflect on what they have done to others which also makes them afraid to face their victims.

Still, ten years after the incident, they meet. And as the conference goes on, there's a softening. The monster becomes much more human and the victims much less judgmental. The victim still has horrible consequences that won't go away, so healing is limited, but the victim does forgive and hugs the one who wounded her at the end of the meeting.

Most victims of abuse mainly find healing and meaning in their walks with God, but the restorative process can help. Wayne Alderson found that the owners had sinned and betrayed him, but were also human. If the perpetrator's story had been told, we may have heard that the captains of industry were caught in the wheels of a system that valued profits over people. We may have heard that, yes, they had a responsibility to do the right and just thing, but also that the devil's world system played a significant part perpetuating injustice, and that everyone needs deliverance *from* injustice as well as empowerment *to be* just. Maybe there was a greater need for a restorative conference than actually happened. God may do that in the final judgment. Everyone will give an account of their lives and all of our stories will be told as we stand before God. We will all see our need for God's grace and redemption, as well as our need for justice, truth, and a new world that has God's order established in it.

✳✳✳✳

There are great stories of whole systems being redeemed like in South Africa, where Nelson Mandela played a significant leadership role in the reconciliation of his country. He clearly believed that injustice was morally wrong and that justice would lead to peace. He also brought an unusual amount of grace to the table, saying, "To make peace with an enemy, one must work with that enemy, and that enemy becomes one's partner."[63] Mandela, like Alderson, granted value to people who did not necessarily earn that value. Even though he was abused by ruling whites, he said, "Whites are fellow South Africans . . . and we want them to feel safe and to know we appreciate the contribution that they have made. . . ."[64] In the end, Mandela said that unity was his goal and that, to be trusted, he had to be committed to both sides. He said, "there was a middle ground between white fears and black hopes." Through a lot of suffering, sacrifice, service, and growth, he brought the nation together.

The goal of faith is love. The order of love is justice, and injustice stands against love. What if you are the one who is victimized? How do you love and bring about justice when you lack power to protect yourself?

---

63  Mandela, 612.
64  Ibid., 568.

When people personally experience the atrocities of injustice they are often motivated to make sacrifices that bring redemption and grace. These stories of how grace *produces* justice are a part of history, and there are so many good true stories of an unjust situation becoming just.

For example, racial injustice has been one of the main themes in this book, and faith has been a transformative force for racial justice. In the early days of our country, an African American slave named Richard Allen was saved. As he became aware of Scripture and the application of trusting God, he became a submissive slave who won his master's heart because of his love for God. He then led his master to Christ. As this slave owner grew in Christ and learned to obey the King, he decided to release Richard Allen from slavery. Allen started the African Methodist Episcopal Church, the first African American national church in America. He became an educator, minister, and writer. His story is an amazing story! There is no guarantee that because a person applies their faith that the promises of God will be experienced in their lifetime, but many have received God's promises as they have called out to God and walked in faith by trusting and obeying their King.

I use this example because racial injustice is or has become a moral standard culturally to measure a person's goodness. Racial injustice is wrong, but so is any sin that a person or group commits. We are all sinners. Our value comes from God, who empowers us to be moral in all areas of His Kingdom as we grow in our faith. Racial morality is one of the areas where God can and does bring transformation.

Our only true value comes from the love of God, which is redemptive and, by its very nature, makes the wrongs of this life right. It is not a cultural morality that makes us good or bad but the divine nature granted through the life of Christ. God takes our mistakes and losses and, through faith, makes the bad into something good.

God is faithful and works all things together for good, and Wayne's job loss called him into mission and ministry in a new way. Wayne started a ministry to train and teach others about the value of the person. Christ's Kingdom is not here yet. Only as believers follow His rule on earth as it is in heaven, will it be manifest in grace communities.

## CONCLUSION

For the Christian, justice is as much about compassion, grace, and equity as it is about accountability and punishment. That is because justice is about the right order of relationships to all things from a Kingdom perspective. It is invited by responding to the King, the Ruler of our lives, and the systems we live in, through a love relationship with Him, others, and ourselves. God Himself defines this order, and to get definitions of that order we have to seek Him and be willing to do His will. This also may take some great Christian thinking in the whole context of the problems that we are experiencing today. We need to be able to exegete both our culture and the Word to see His Kingdom come on earth as it is in heaven.

# ACKNOWLEDGMENTS

I would like to thank Janet Gray for editing this book, for taking the time and effort to make corrections and making it into something readable. Thank you, Janet! I appreciate you very much. I would also like to thank Sarah Hood for her diligence in editing this book, as well as Sarah's brother Cameron Hood for his work on formatting this book. I appreciate so much all the work put into this book by others who have worked to serve its purposes. Thank you and God bless!

# BIBLIOGRAPHY

Boszormeny-Nagy, Ivan, and Geraldine M. Sparks. *Invisible Loyalties*. New York: Brunner/Mazel Publishers, 1984.

Braithwaite, John. *Crime, Shame, and Reintegration*. Cambridge Cambridgeshire; New York, NY: Cambridge University Press, 1989.

Brooks, David. *The Road to Character*. New York: Random House, 2015.

*Christianity Today*. January/February, 2014.

Chernow, Ron. *Washington: A Life*. New York: Penguin Books, 2010.

Collins, James C. *How the Mighty Fall: And Why Some Companies Never Give In*. New York: Jim Collins: Distributed in the U.S. and Canada exclusively by HarperCollins Publishers, 2009.

Collins, James C., and Jerry I. Porras. *Built to Last: Successful Habits of Visionary Companies*. 1st ed. New York: HarperBusiness, 1994.

Cozzens, Peter. *The Earth is Weeping: The Epic Story of the Indian Wars for the American West*. New York: Vintage Books, 2016.

Corbett, Steve, and Brian Fikkert. *When Helping Hurts: How to Alleviate Poverty Without Hurting the Poor—and Yourself*. Chicago: Moody Publishers, 2009.

Gladwell, Malcolm. *Outliers: The Story of Success*. New York: Little, Brown & Co., 2008.

Guinness, Os. *Fit Bodies, Fat Minds: Why Evangelicals Don't Think and What to Do About It*. Grand Rapids, MI: Hourglass Books, 1994.

Hall, Ron, Denver Moore, and Lynn Vincent. *Same Kind of Different As Me*. Nashville: Thomas Nelson, 2006.

Kahn, Roger. *Rickey and Robinson: The True, Untold Story of the Integration of Baseball*. Emmaus: Rodale Books, 2014.

Keller, Timothy J. *Generous Justice: How God's Grace Makes Us Just*. 1st ed. New York: Dutton, Penguin Group USA, 2010.

Kramer, Mark. *Dispossessed: Life in Our World's Urban Slums*. Maryknoll, NY: Orbis Books, 2006.

Mandela, Nelson. *Long Walk to Freedom*. Boston, MA: Little, Brown & Co., 1994.

Mott, Stephen Charles. *Biblical Ethics and Social Change*. New York: Oxford University Press, 1982.

Plantinga, Cornelius. *Not the Way It's Supposed to Be: A Breviary of Sin*. Grand Rapids, MI; Leicester, Eng.: Eerdmans; Apollos, 1995.

Smith, Stephen C. *Ending Global Poverty: A Guide to What Works*. New York: Palgrave Macmillan, 2005.

Sproul, R. C. *Stronger Than Steel: The Wayne Alderson Story.* 1st ed. San Francisco, CA: Harper & Row, 1980.

Stearns, Richard. *The Hole in Our Gospel: What Does God Expect of Us? The Answer That Changed My Life and Might Just Change the World.* Nashville: Thomas Nelson Inc., 2009.

Swanson, Eric and Sam Williams. *To Transform a City.* Grand Rapids, MI: Zondervan, 2010.

Volf, Miroslav. *Exclusion and Embrace: A Theological Exploration of Identity, Otherness, and Reconciliation.* Nashville: Abingdon Press, 1996.

Wilkerson, Isabel. *The Warmth of Other Suns: The Epic Story of America's Great Migration.* New York: Vintage Books, 2010.

Winston, Diane H. *Red-Hot and Righteous: The Urban Religion of the Salvation Army.* Cambridge, MA: Harvard University Press, 1999.

Yancey, Philip. *Soul Survivor: How My Faith Survived the Church.* 1st ed. New York: Doubleday, 2001.

Yunus, Mohammad. *Banker to the Poor: Micro-lending and the Battle Against World Poverty in the United States.* New York: PublicAffairs, 2003.

Zehr, Howard. *Changing Lenses: A New Focus for Crime and Justice.* 3rd ed. Scottdale, PA: Herald Press, 2005.